An Irish Nurse

Maureen Ryan

Maureen Ryan nee Fergus,

date of birth 26th of February 1934.

ISBN: 9798440251144

This book is memoir. It reflects the author's present recollections
of experiences over time. Some names have been changed to
protect privacy. Although the author has made every effort to
ensure that the information in this book was correct at press time,
the author does not assume and hereby disclaims any liability to
any party for any loss, damage, or disruption caused by errors or
omissions, whether such errors or omissions result from
negligence, accident, or any other cause.

"I'm going back to Ireland in the morning,

I'm going to walk Lough Melvin's rocky shore"

John Farry, *Lough Melvin's Rocky Shore,* 1986

CONTENTS

Foreword

My mother often told little snippets of stories of her life; even recently at the age of 88 she recalled events I had never heard before. On a visit one day, I suggested that she just write down some headings for topics she might later write about, such as *Early Memories of Childhood* and *First Nursing Days in England*, to be ready for the following week. Two days later on the phone she told me she had written twelve pages! These flowed in a stream of consciousness, or more like a river, spanning her eight decades, often on a single page. Over the next couple of months, more memories were gathered and handed over, some swirling like little eddies, often returning to add detail and colour to earlier recorded images, others bubbling over the recent torrent of changes caused by the lockdown, whilst always abounding with energy. At times the memories were like the ebb and flow of the tide: a section would start with an early memory, yet its telling would collect up with it reflections of more recent times, and vice versa. In order to help others to navigate this flow, the river's banks have been mapped through headings and a gentle time line, to enable you to bob along a life well lived.

Katharine Ryan-Murray, Daughter. February 2022

An Irish Nurse

Preface

Whenever I asked my Mam about her earlier life, she would always say, "I'll tell you later", but she never did. This book is dedicated to my grandsons, Joel and Peter, so they will know about their Granny's life, and may be surprised along the way.

1 INTRODUCTIONS: PEOPLE AND PLACES

My Names

I was christened 'Mary Bernadette'. When I was a baby Mam and Dad had a maid, and whatever way she called out to me my grandmother hated the sound of it, and changed my name to Maureen, which I like. At school I was called 'Maura'. During my student training I was called 'Fergus'. After I was married, as a student in Goodmayes we had to sign a book in the assistant matron's office. On a few occasions I signed 'Fergus', but soon got used to my new name. The change from Mary to Maureen was never done legally so if I have to sign something such as cheques, which I don't do now, or for my medical records, it's Mary Bernadette Ryan.

My Parents and Grandparents

My Dad (1), Charles Joseph Fergus was born in 1906 in the townland of Uragh, Tullaghan, in County Leitrim, in the west of Ireland. They may have gone to the USA for a while. My dad was an only child, and by photographs in my possession, his parents, Hugh Fergus and Mary (nee McGowan) seemed for those days quite well off. In the census of 1911 when my Dad was 5, Hugh Fergus was 58,

Mary was 43, and they are recorded as having three servants. Hugh Fergus, my grandfather, owned a large area of turf at Uragh, and to this day it is known as "Fergus bog". I have got some turf from there, in a bag in the garage at Aughavoghill given to Tim, my husband by Willy Clancy, known locally as 'the bachelor'.

'Mother'

My maternal grandmother whom we had to call 'Mother', Mary Jane McClean, was also a qualified nurse. Her father, my great grandfather was Francis McClean, the man in the top hat! Kathleen Coll, a first cousin, told me that my maternal grandfather, Peter Gormley, was a rent or tax collector and cleared off to Canada with all the cash and did not return. I asked Mam about her dad: "I'll tell you sometimes", she said, but she never did. However, on the marriage certificate for Mam's brother Joseph in 1925, Peter Gormley's profession is recorded as 'grocer'. Joseph's son Vincent Gormley did some work on the family tree, stating that Peter went to America to work, stayed in touch with Mary Jane by letter, though infrequently, and died in America on 7th November 1959 (2).

Catherine Gormley, Mam

My mother, Catherine Gormley was born in Drumquin, Omagh, Co. Tyrone on the 10th of January 1904.

She had two sisters and two brothers, and was educated at Hughes Academy in Belfast. I'm still in contact with her nephews, my cousins Vincent and John Gormley, both in their 90s. Vincent lives in Drogheda and John lives in Muff. One sister, Agnes, was a nun in the Poor Clares religious order. She was very ill at some stage of her life and was allowed home from the convent to recover. She did make a recovery and was out on her bike when she was knocked down by an oil lorry and died from her injuries. Another sister, Gertrude was a nurse, and died of typhoid. I did know Mam's sister, my aunt Minnie, who was married, and I have a photo taken with her. Her brother, my Uncle Joe, in later life had a pub, The Ture Inn, in Donegal. He and his wife Essie sold the pub to the singer, Dana. She won the Eurovision Song Contest for Ireland in 1970. Eddie, another brother went to Canada. Mam tried to trace him via priests, and got a reply only from the Salvation Army, and they said he may have been murdered. She said they were the only ones that helped her. If I see the Salvation Army now, I always give them money because of that. Vincent Gormley's family tree work found that Eddie became a trapper and prospector for gold/ uranium and died in Nova Scotia around 1950. There is more searching to be done!

Benedict Kiely, writer and broadcaster was my Mam's first cousin. I went to his funeral in Omagh to represent the family, and Seamus Heaney, poet, gave a fifteen-minute oration for him. Mam would never talk about Benedict Kiely because of the content of his books, that she did not approve of (Three of his early novels were banned under Irish censorship laws, since repealed). In his later book, *Drink to the Bird,* Kiely looks back over his life, recalls various relatives including "Uncles Dan and Peter who were legends" (3). This was my grandfather, Peter, married to Mary Jane. Kiely noted that there were many Gormleys in the locality, who, like the Ryans in Tipperary (Tim Ryan was a 'Ryan Darby') used nicknames to distinguish between them. These are the 'Múinte Gormleys' which means in English, "Taught, instructed, educated, learned, polite, good-mannered". Benedict Kiely, as anyone would be, was happy with that description!

Vincent Gormley's son John Joseph, my Mam's great nephew became Lord Mayor of Dublin, and later Minister for the Environment when the Green Party joined a Coalition Government with the Fianna Fail Party.

The Nurse and the Farmer

Mam had been working in an office in Belfast and decided to take up nursing in Newcastle upon Tyne, England. Her brother Joe was working there from 1925-1931, so maybe that was the reason she went over. Her mother, my maternal grandmother had a lot of property there and may have done her nursing there previously. Mam got her SRN (State Registered Nurse) in Newcastle Royal Infirmary, and then qualified as a midwife in Batley Hospital, Yorkshire 23rd February 1929. After Mam was trained, and before she was married, she got a job in Omagh as a matron. She thought that because of her religion, being a Catholic, she would not get the job, but she did. She was the first Catholic matron in the whole of Northern Ireland, staying in post until she married. Dad and Mam both had relatives in County Tyrone (McQuaids) and that is how they met in their young days, so at this stage Mam and Dad were well acquainted. Dad carried on as a farmer in Uragh after the death of his parents. Dad used to go to Omagh, get a white coat and go and see her in the hospital! The other staff thought he was a doctor.

They married on the 22nd of September 1932, the year of the Roman Catholic Church Eucharistic Congress. Her mother arranged all the wedding and didn't ask many people, as you can see from the wedding photo. They married in Saint Eugene's Cathedral in Derry. My nephew Marc Geagan, Pat's son and teacher of music in Derry, recently took a group of students to the Cathedral and told them of the family connection. Their Reception was in the Guildhall in Derry. Barney McGowan, first cousin of Dad, was best man. He is the father of Tony and Brian from Bundoran BMG, Hardware Store. My Mam would sometimes say, "Around here, the dog is related to the cat".

When Mam and Dad returned after their wedding (did they have a honeymoon I wonder?), there were tar barrels lit from the village of Kinlough to Uragh- about 2 miles. Mam said it was a wonderful sight.

From Uragh to Stracomer via Bundoran
When I was a baby in Uragh, my Mam told me that I had to be given goat's milk instead of cow's milk. My Dad didn't have goats on the farm, so he had to travel a distance to obtain goats milk from another farmer.

In the early years of marriage, Dad was given the Stracomer house and farm by his uncle, Patrick Fergus (1851-1934). Patrick Fergus was a prominent man in the Land League struggle, chairman of the old Ballyshannon Board of Guardians, a member of Leitrim County Council, and Governor of the Shiel Hospital in Ballyshannon. At that time, Stracomer was occupied by Mary McQuaid (a sister to Peter McQuaid, cousins of my Dad) and Thomas Fergus, another cousin, and they were asked to vacate the property. While this was going on, Mam and Dad moved to Shell House in Bundoran and did Bed & Breakfast there. Aidan was born whilst they lived in Shell House. They already had three children- Me-Maureen, Teresa and Hugh. Whilst living in the Shell House, my Dad and a friend were looking after me one day when I was about three. They took me down to the beach, and they lost me! My Dad found me and told me about it years later. A young man came back from America, where his wife had died, with his three young children, and bought Uragh. While in Uragh Mam set a rose bush at the door. She brought Tim Ryan and I to see it one day years ago. I wonder if it is still there. The house was later bought by a man by the name of Feeley. I went again to see the house with Katharine, Tim Murray and the boys. I was unable to get over the gate- Katharine will remember that. Mam and Dad moved into Stracomer in 1936.

Francis McClean. Maternal Great Grandfather

**Mary Jane,
Maternal
Grandmother**

Dad and Paternal Grandparents, Hugh and Mary

Mary McGowan, Paternal Grandmother

Mam (right) with siblings Joe, Eddie, Agnes, Gertrude

Mam

Dad

Mam and Dad's Wedding 1932. Back left to right Uncle Joe Gormley, Aunt Essie, Priest, Mary Jane, Dad, Mam, Priest. Front left to right Tommy Hanahoe (1st cousin to Mam), Minnie Gormley, Gertrude Gormley, Barney McGowan (1st cousin to Dad)

Shell House: photograph courtesy of National Inventory of Architectural Heritage

2 STRACOMER THEN AND NOW

Our House

Stracomer is the name of the townland, the house and farm. The historical spelling was 'Sracummer' as in the 1851 census of Ireland (see map). It stretched from Breffni to Pat Hughie's land down to the lake. The following passage, reproduced in full from *The Schools Collection* at Duchas.ie, a project to digitize the Irish National Folklore Collection (4), has the following story below, as told by Owen Meehan, aged 77, from Buckode, County Leitrim and collected by Gerard Haran, Bomahas, Co Leitrim. It shows the importance locally of the farm in the history of the 'faith of our fathers'.

An Altar Stone

During the penal times about one hundred and fifty years ago the parishes of Glenade, Kinlough, and Ballaghmeehan were one parish and that parish was called Rossinver. There was only one chapel in the parish and one priest whose name was Curneen. The chapel was situated in the townland of Aughamore. This priest was hated very much by the Protestants especially by the Johnstons of Kinlough and he was not allowed to say mass in the chapel. This priest did a thing which the Johnstons disliked very much. He married a lady of the Johnstons to a man named McGloin who owned the townland of Bloonawilliam.

Then the Johnstons wished to punish the priest and they pursued him day and night. The only place where this priest got any refuge was in the town lands of Stracomer and Buckode. At that time there was a great view from a field in Patrick Fergus's farm and he gave permission to read mass on a stone. The reason why mass was said in this field was because there was a great view from it and the foe could be seen approaching. There was a number of trees growing around the field now and the view is not as good as it was when mass was read in it. Father Burneen never was caught by the Johnstons and he died a natural death.

A large stone, we always referred to as 'The Long Stone', was maybe the altar stone.

In the house, Mam and Dad now had seven children: Mary Bernadette(me), Teresa, Hugh, Aiden, Gertrude (Gertie), Cathal (Irish for Charles), and Patricia (Pat). We had a very good upbringing with religion very much 'top norm'. The rosary was said each night and had to be stopped often as we were all laughing. We were all given piano lessons, with the teacher coming to the house. I still wonder how did they afford that? Mark Geagan still has that piano in his house and is very proud to have it.

The Lake and Around

As children we would go to the lake, Lough Melvin, and catch daddy longlegs for the fishermen. They would give us sweets. The lake was a great thing for the farmers who had land on the lake shore. The cattle in warm weather would go for a drink in the lake.

Aidan, my younger brother was always doing things. One time the lake was frozen, and he took Gertie out to the island walking across the ice. My parents got to know this and there was "No Lake" after that. We were told stories that the

Dobhar-chú (5) and Banshee (a fairy woman whose wailing warned of a death) were there at the lake, to keep us away. We used to listen to the Banshee crying and knew that was a sign somebody was drowned. There were people drowned in that lake. There was a lot of smuggling on the lake- cattle for example: "There's more than cattle going on that boat", I remember someone saying. We saw the cattle being made to swim behind boats from farms in the south into the North, where they would get more money for them. During that time, it was known people were drowned whilst smuggling cattle.

We picked sloes and put them in jam jars, and buried them for nine days. They were supposed to produce sloe wine. There are plenty buried around Stracomer, never to be found.

Donkeys, Horses and Other Animals

Us girls never did any farming work; the boys did the milking, looked after the calves and the horses. As children in Stracomer we had a donkey. Most farmers had one. I think they said it was to keep the cows happy. Two of us would get on its back and the rest would be pushing it to make it walk -poor animal. It never kicked us so docile. We were told stories about why the donkey had a cross on its back, as it carried Jesus to Jerusalem, and then witnessed Him on the Cross (6)

I remember Cathal, my brother, as a child sitting in the field with a weasel beside him. Hedges were never cut before September to enable the wild birds to nest. We did go looking for birds' nests. We did not know that if you went near the nest, the birds would not come back.

I remember going to the forge with my Dad to get the horse shod. The first time, I got very upset to see the red-hot shoe being put on the horse, because as a child I was unaware that the horse did not feel this. After that I liked going to the Forge with my Dad.

As a child I remember Dad telling us that his Uncle Patrick bred racehorses at Stracomer. This interest in horses was continued in the equestrian school commenced by Terri, then passed on to Pat. Many nieces and nephews in the various families do horse-riding, even those living in England. I remember as a child my brothers Hugh, Aidan, Cahal standing up and riding bareback! I did ask Terri if I could go down to her Riding School. Well, I think I was put on the biggest horse she could find: that was the end of me and horse-riding!

In Sheffield, I've just been to an alpaca farm with Katharine: a very interesting place with a lot of animals there, but I now know I'm not keen on alpacas! One was particularly unfriendly, and kept hissing at us. Apparently, they are good at protecting chickens from foxes.

Saving the Turf

Turf cutting in our young days was essential to keep us warm and for the cooking. My Dad cut the turf with a special two-sided spade called a 'sleán'- there is one in the garage in Aughavohill that Tim got from somewhere. As children we all went up to 'the resting place', as it was called, on the road to the bog. There is a wonderful view from there, back down over the lake. We went up through the fields to wait for Dad to come up. I do remember Tim and I got turf cut by machine, and we went to the bog to 'save' the turf. I think we met up with Hugh and family, built a fire, boiled the kettle and had a great meal. The tea had a great taste. I suppose it was the water from the river. In the bog, if you were lucky, you could find bog oak. This was the remains of ancient pine trees which covered Ireland thousands of years ago. In Aughavohill there is a lot of turf still there. It will be able to keep Joel and Peter warm in future years. We always brought a bag back to Sheffield for Christmas and Tim Murray loved to see it. There is a piece of bog oak in Aughavohill painted in black. Years ago, there was a lovely piece in the Great Northern Hotel. I wonder if it is still there. The government in Ireland are now trying to stop turf cutting, to reduce carbon emissions and protect the rare habitats.

Family Life and Visitors

Going back to my childhood in Stracomer, electricity was not in any house. My Mam got gas lights erected. The radio was on a wet battery- how was it re-filled; I wonder?

The roof was thatched and one day while dad was away, the house caught fire. There was no Fire Brigade in those days. All the neighbours carried the water from the lake and put out the fire as Dad came on the scene. "Boys you did a great job", he said. They were all brought in for a good meal and maybe drinks. Before water was in the house it was carried from a deep well. The field was called "The Well Field"; it was covered as it was dangerous for small children.

Some more things come into my head…. in the evenings we were all got ready for bed and all bathed in a big bath in front of the fire to keep us warm. No central heating in those days, and there was no tap water in the house. I always got in first as I was the eldest, and it was the same water for all; some taken out and warm water put in. I always remember that ordeal. Dad got water plumbed in later and a nice bathroom.

I remember a saying from my Dad: "I spent all these years keeping the water out and now you see what Mam has done, and brought the water in". My dad then told us stories before we went off to bed: ghost stories sometimes, and we were all frightened!

The sitting room has now been turned into a bedroom. We were never allowed to go there; visitors were taken there. We all had a night in turn to stay up and you would count yourself lucky if visitors came on your night. There was a full set of Belleek China on the table in there. It belonged to Dad's parents.

I well remember this family of Irish Travellers coming to the house. They always arrived when the dinner was ready, and they were always given a lovely hot meal. The father with them used to make 'pongers' (larger than a cup, and had a handle). He also made buckets or small things to carry water. Mam and Dad were very kind to them. I often wondered what happened to them. They had a lot of small children and came on regular visits.

The post man, Dano Warnock, always got tea and boiled eggs when he came. He was on his bike; I remember there were carbon lights on bikes; now they have van transport.

Orchards and Around
Mam and Dad always had a maid to help look after the children, and I remember some of them. One married Bernard Connolly and owned the house where Charlie, Hugh's son and his wife Claire live now. Mam and Dad went out a lot to whist drives and visiting people. The rambling houses were common. The house at Aughavoghill, which we later bought, was top, especially when owned by Rooney

family. Kevin O'Reilly, our neighbour, told me that.

When Mam and Dad went to mass, and we were too young to go, the maid was left looking after us. We all went robbing orchards: there were a lot in those days. We even went to Hugh Charlie's orchard, which is now the field at Aughavohill where Joel and Peter used to play, and where Tim built them a tree house. Hugh Charlie got us and marched us home, so that was the end of that. How did we get that far from home? Up the fields, I suppose, with my brother Aidan leading the pack. There were two shops on the road: one owned by Barney and Mai McGowan, and the second was McCabes. Barney McGowan was my dad's first cousin, and it was in this house that my paternal grandmother, Mary was born. Both houses are derelict now. Well, I can't think of any more.

The Neighbours, the Fairies and the Fairy Neighbours
On the lane down to the house at Stracomer, you will see the "fort" (7) on the left, with holly and other bushes growing on it. We were always told never to destroy this fort. Wherever there was a fairy tree in the fields, they were (and still are) not to be damaged, because to do so would bring you bad luck.

There was a house at the top of the lane owned by Denny Sheerhan. It is now Kevin's, our neighbour's, as Kevin's wife was a niece of Denny's. Denny always gave Katharine two and six and once she demanded it from him on our way back to England! That was a lot of money in those days. He always came down to Stracomer to 'ramble' or 'cuairt', in Irish (8). One night my brothers -probably including Aiden, as he was always up to tricks, got a flash lamp in the fort and frightened the life out of Denny. He ran all the way down and told Mam

and Dad that the fairies were in the fort. He was EXHAUSTED. He was given tea and maybe poteen (9). He refused to go back up the lane; my Dad brought him home.

**John Haran,
Denny Sheerhan,
Gerard Haran**

I remember Dad telling us about "getting lost" himself near there. It was in a field going down on the left of the lane. He was coming from somewhere and just could not get home? He may have stayed there for some time; he did tell us but I've forgotten. There were stories about fairies confusing the local people just going about their business.

When I was a child there was another house near Stracomer. It was owned by John Gilroy (10), a retired American. When he went to town on his donkey and cart, he always brought us sweets. He would say to dad, "Charlie I brought candy for the children". He died and eventually the house was turned into a byre for the cows and Mam kept the hens there, which never got let out. They were supposed to lay twice a day. Then when Hugh and Rita married, they had it done up as a nice house again. The Schools Collection at <u>Duchas.ie</u>, a project to digitize the Irish National Folklore Collection from the 1930s, has the following story below, again told by Owen Meehan, and collected by Gerard Haran:

A Giant

Scattered here and there throughout this district are graves of giants. Once upon a time there lived a giant near Hugh McSharry's house Aughavohill Kinlough Co. Leitrim.

Once a Landlord who lived in Manorhamilton sent thirteen men with swords and spears to kill him. It was on a snowy winters night and when they reached this district they were covered with snow.

When the giant heard them coming, he put out the light and he spilled a pan of cream on himself so that he would not be known from his enemy.

Then he stood behind the door until the men came in. They were fully armed but they thought he was one of their own men. When all the men were in he stood in the middle of the crowd and he killed the last of the thirteen men in his home at the side of the alt. It is also said that the rocks which are in Lake Melvin were thrown out there by the giant to show his strength. He died some years after and was buried in a fort in John Gilroy's land Stracomer, Kinlough, Co. Leitrim. There is a big flag placed over his grave thousands of tons in weight. It is believed locally that there is a pot of gold buried along with him.

'Mother', Mam and Headaches

Our maternal grandmother, 'Mother', was a business woman all her life in pubs and owned a lot of property in Newcastle in England. I remember Dad went to help her in the last one she had in Rossgeir, Lifford, County Donegal, and remember meeting him on the lane coming home from school. I always remember he had a bike with him, and wonder how did he get to Rossgeir way up in Donegal? While he was up there, Mam did all the farm work, and there was no machinery in those days. She suffered a lot from headaches and I can picture her with a scarf covering on her head. "Mrs Cullen's Powders" (with active ingredients Aspirin and caffeine) was always top on the shopping list.

Mam made a lot of our clothes: she was a good dressmaker (Katharine carried this on skill, studying Needlework at school and made me a lot of summer dresses.) We were always well dressed. Some first cousin sent nice clothes (hand-me downs), but Dad had them returned.

Another bit of history: later on, my Mam was noted for reading the cups. Whether she could or not, I don't know. If we were out amongst people, they would say, "Mrs Fergus, read my cup", and she did, and explained what she read in the leaves.

Food

As a child, as we had a farm, all vegetables were home grown. A pig was not kept to be killed as previously, a pig had got swine fever on the farm, and it was a government ruling that after this happened you were not allowed to keep pigs. Breakfast was porridge, then all had eggs, bread and butter. Fried food was rare. We had our own hens, so we always had plenty of eggs. Dinner was potatoes and vegetables, with meat from the butcher. Potatoes were boiled in a large pot. Mam was great at making potato cakes and 'boxtie' (made from raw potatoes). If potatoes were leftover, as was always the case, Mam would peel and mash them up with salt and flour to make potato cakes. This was wonderful: As you can imagine seven of us were waiting to get our share. For the making of 'Boxtie', raw potatoes were grated, then mixed with flour and salt, which looked like pancakes and was delicious. Mam made her own butter in the churn. We always wanted a chance to churn a few times so there was always plenty of butter. (In later years when we were in Tipperary, Tim would always buy a supply of butter from a shop in Nenagh and bring it back to Gresham Drive.)

Memorable Trips

When Dad was away helping our grandmother, Mam would take us all off to Bundoran in the pony and trap. One day the trap got too near to the bridge outside Kinlough. The pony went berserk, rearing up on its hind legs, but Mam sorted it out. I always remember that day when we cross Lennox's Bridge in the car now.

As a child I remember Mam and Dad going away down Donegal once, with us in the car. Dad was watching the petrol gauge dropping, but knew where there was a garage at "Biddy of Barnes" pub at Barnesmore Gap. We got there and I remember that night he was knocking on the door for ages and no reply. We got home eventually- I will never forget that night.

It was War Time

I remember when we were young there was great excitement when a plane crashed on the far side of the lough at Askill. It was 30 April 1941, when I was seven. The plane was flying the 'Donegal corridor' route that included north Leitrim, as a shortcut to the Atlantic. The men in it all survived the crash and fled across the border on foot. Many people including us lot went to see where it came down; Dad took us over there in the horse and trap, and we collected bits of the plane. In the end he declared, "no more pieces of plane thank you"! War had come this near, but we were never aware of the horrors of it. On 23 January 1944, the aircrew of a Halifax bomber were not so lucky when they struck the cliff at Fairy Bridges, Bundoran, Co. Donegal, when all ten died, with four washed out to sea.

Mam the Midwife. Births and Loss

Mam took up the post of midwife in the Kinlough area in 1948, when Pat was young. Joe Gallagher was her first baby (11). She went off on her bike, hail, rain or snow when

needed, with of course no lights like we have now, and had a large area to cover. Mam had a basket on the front, in which she kept a lot of bones. This was because so many people had dogs and they ran after people on bikes and maybe would do damage to you. Mum gave them bones! One baby she delivered was only 1lb. in weight. She went to a bike shop and bought some kind of rubber tube and valve. She put the rubber tube into the baby and fed it. She would go off each day on her bike to feed the baby. The baby grew up to be a big man and maybe had children of his own. She was district midwife for twenty-one years, until her retirement in 1969.

In later years Veronica, my niece and godchild who is a nurse, spent time in Abu Dhabi, United Arab Emirates, and when she returned to Ireland, the carers who looked after

Mam were going on holiday, so Veronica took their place. Of course, Mam was delighted with Veronica as she was also a qualified nurse. Mam told Veronica that years ago if a baby was stillborn, the baby was not allowed to be buried in consecrated ground. It must have been sad for the parents. My mam's nursing bag and that of her mother, Mary Jane were put into the Kinlough Museum for safekeeping. I have often gone in to see them. There are no names on either article.

A lot of things come into my head and I would like to share them with you all. My Mam-RIP, only told us bits of her life and I don't want to do that. I was the first born to Mam and Dad. She did let slip that she had lost twins before I was born. She didn't tell this to anybody else for years. I did ask her if they were boys or girls, but she refused to disclose this. Since coming to Sheffield, my niece Veronica now living in Ireland, said "Granny did tell me she had twins, Auntie Maureen". I'm glad that she spoke of it. Lots of nieces and nephews have been blessed with twins- there are four sets now.

Years ago, we went to a 'benefit' dance (fundraiser) for Kinlough Community Centre, held in London. Mam was at that time living with us. She came and all the folk from home gave her a great welcome. A photo was taken and is now on show in the Community Centre.

A story
I had a cousin, Peter McQuaid, who owned a pub in Kinlough that later became McGloin's. He was related to my Dad, and his wife Theresa was related to my Mam. They are buried in the old graveyard in Kinlough. Peter would go to town on his pony and trap, and drink and drink. He would

not drink in his own pub. Wherever he was drinking, he was well known, and the owner of the pub would put him in his trap and the pony would take him home safely. I well remember as a child my Dad would leave his horse and trap outside McQuaid's pub in the pub yard. After mass we were given pennies and off we went to Sadie Dudigan's and got sweets.

McQuaid's shop in Kinlough

In later years
Stracomer passed to my brother Hugh, the eldest boy and then was divided by him between his sons. At Stracomer Hugh set up a caravan   park where the caravans are owned by families, mostly from Northern Ireland. They have to abide by strict rulings, and if they are not kept to, they get notice to leave. The park was closed during the Lockdown due to the virus (Covid 2019). Water is provided by Hugh Og, via a water system. Gas is bottled and brought in Kinlough.

I'm doing a lot more thinking: it is indeed nice to know that our family home is still owned by "Mr and Mrs Fergus": Hugh Óg (son of Hugh and Rita) and Martina and it is kept very nice. They have two children, Sadhbh and Fionn.

I remember going for a drive up the Glan Road quite recently- the road up behind the mountain that goes to the bog: all around there were so many houses derelict. We got out and looked in the windows: it looked like the people had got up from the table and just left -cups and saucers still on the table. I wonder where did they go?

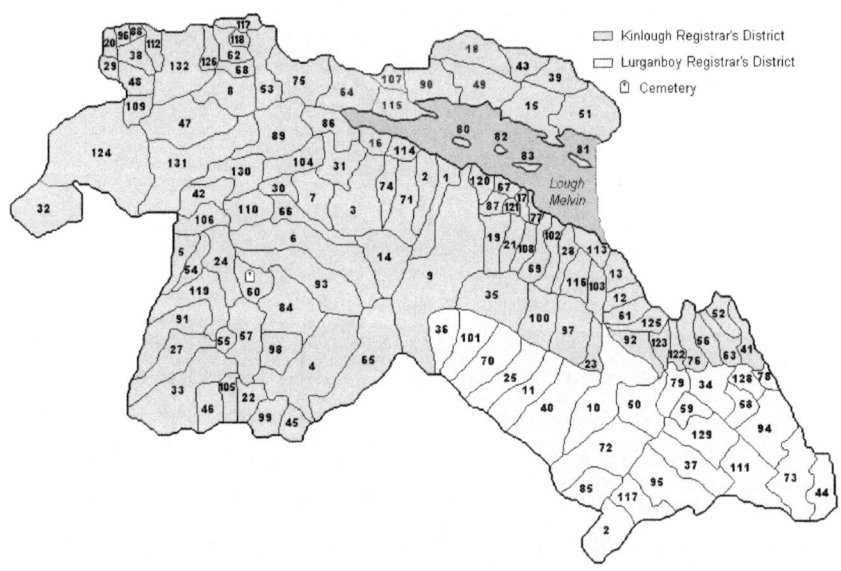

Stracomer/ Sracummer townland 120, Aughavoghil 9.
Map for the Civil Parish of Rossinver in County Leitrim (leitrim-roscommon.com)

An Irish Nurse

3 BELIEFS AND TRADITIONS

As a child, religion in our household was a top priority. There was mass each Sunday and the Rosary was said each night, which as I said sometimes ended up with a good telling off as we got a fit of laughing, putting an end to the Rosary. I may have mentioned this: "Never say anything bad about a priest". It was bad luck. I always remember that from Mam and Dad and keep to it.

Masses were said in the country houses by the parish priest. These were called "The Stations" (12). Before this would happen, there were great preparations. The place would all be painted -white wash for outside, and cleaned. A lot of people came, and the Stations entailed confession, mass, a money collection for the priest and a good breakfast.

Special Days
I remember both First Communion and Confirmation in Kinlough. I remember walking back from Kinlough with Terri and Hugh after our First Holy Communion. Terri and I were in our white dresses. John Foley, the taxi driver picked us up and brought us home. I wonder if he was paid by Mam

and Dad?

Christmas to us as small children was a great event. My Dad dressed up in full Christmas dress and with a hat: we didn't recognise him. We got presents- not too big, but we were all excited.

In Ireland on Saint Stephen's Day (26th December) the 'Wren boys' would dress up: changing their appearance with old ragged clothes, painting their faces, then go around the houses singing, playing music and collecting money, asking the householders to "give us a penny to bury the 'wran'(wren). It was an ancient tradition going back centuries (13). I don't know what they did with the money.

There were a lot of dances around Christmas in particular country houses. We were allowed to go to Kelly's, as it was nearby, and I remember Maurice Kelly being there. I well remember going to them- it was a great time, with all the locals there. We went in and danced around like 'egits'. Musicians knew where the dances were and they always played for free. They were called 'Mummers dances' (14). You got tea, soft drinks and something to eat, but no alcohol. All that has now stopped. Ireland has changed a lot -for the better I suppose.

On Easter Sunday, as well as going to mass, we built 'Easter houses' and boiled eggs to see which of us could eat the most (15). Believe me, it always rained on Easter Sunday.

While children in Stracomer, on the 1st of May we were sent out in the field to collect 'May flowers' to put them on all the windowsills and where the animals were. It was supposed to bring good luck.

The Cure

There are many people who have The Cure all over Ireland. It is used a lot for nearly everything that occurs, such as shingles, warts: and no matter where you had a pain, especially in your back, you would go to someone for The Cure (16). I did go once, but can't remember if it worked. Indeed, I could go now as my back is in constant pain. The person who had The Cure that I knew of first, was Nan Rooney (first cousin of my Dad). It was handed to her by her husband Phil. They are all gone now: RIP. She gave it to a daughter. Now if you want The Cure, you go to Noel McGowan. He has a large ball of wool, given to him by the Rooney family. When I got The Cure, it consisted of a large piece of wool put around my waist, never to be taken off. I kept it on for many years. No money was exchanged for this. It still goes on in Ireland a lot and especially with the elderly and young.

I've been reading *The Things We Handed Down,* by Colman Rushe (17), and some of the Cures were ones I've seen done: To prevent needing to go to the vet, which was very expensive, animals were inspected for ticks and parasites. If any were found, when the animal urinated, the urine was collected and put in a whiskey bottle, and this was dosed to the animal. No money was requested: a glass of whiskey was given. I knew these too: if you had a wound, it was thought that dog saliva would cure the wound. Plaster the wound with a lot of butter to encourage the dog to lick the wound. If you have warts, wait for a rainy day and go up the hill hoping that the rain would leave pockets of water in stones. Sit down and rub this water onto your warts. A great success.

4 TO SCHOOL

Buckode School and Beyond

We all went to Buckode National School at the top of the lane from Stracomer. It was a two-teachers school. Some teachers stayed in lodgings with Mam and Dad. The teachers were Miss Coyle and Master Fitzgerald. They were very kind and good, but then moved to Kinlough. Miss Coyle did have some unusual ideas though. She believed that the Blessed Virgin Mary would appear up behind the school and gave us teaspoons to dig with to see if we could find her…Then it was Maurice McFadden from Donegal. The parents of the children in the school gave the turf for the school fire. We all had to carry the turf to the hall. At lunchtime we were put out in the grounds, "hail, rain or snow" while the teachers sat at a lovely fire. We did not like that as we all knew that our parents had provided the turf.

The toilet was up behind the school – a small construction built over the river. You went in there, did your business and let it run away with the water below. No flush loos. We were always sent off to school with shoes and socks on. Before going in though, we took them off on the lane, as some children didn't have shoes to wear. Sometimes we would forget where we left them!

If it was your turn to get a slap at school, you would pull a piece of hair and put it on your hand. I don't know if it made any difference.

I remember as a child if anyone came into the school in uniform, priest or Garda (Irish police force), I would run out and run home down the lane-why, I don't know. I must have been very nervous as a child.

As we came in from school all clothes were taken off and washed, as there were a lot of children with lice. All hair was rubbed with paraffin oil and combed to remove anything that we may have got. It was not a pleasant ordeal especially for me with curly hair. A few tears were shed.

The old school was closed up for many years, then later sold by the church and bought by Cathal, my brother. Hugh and Rita, his wife, bought it from Cathal and had a lovely home built by the Rynn brothers. Rita, Pauline my niece and her son Fiacra, still live there.

'Mother', Sea Creatures and Donegal
After my grandmother, 'Mother', retired I was sent to keep her company, maybe from the age of eight to fourteen years old. She moved around a lot and her houses were always comfortable. I was very happy with her, though I remember she was strict. I enjoyed it and met a lot of friends. Though I spent many years with my grandmother, I do remember having great times with my brothers and sisters.

When I first went, my grandmother was living in Drung, a

village and townland near Quigley's Point in Donegal, close to her son Joe's home. During my stay near the seafront in Drung, my friends and I would go to the seashore and catch some sea creatures- periwinkles. We always were told to bring a tin with us; then we would light a fire and cook them. We could watch big liners going up and down the sea; where they were going to, we never did ask, and nobody told us (18). There was a pub in Drung, and I got friendly with their daughter. Some years ago, Dad (Tim Ryan) and I did go back to Drung and made contact with those people, but I have now lost contact.

A Young Smuggler Served Mass, and was Witness to the End of the Battle of the Atlantic

The last place I remember living with my grandmother was Carrigans outside Derry (19). Carrigans is in Southern Ireland. I went to school by bus across the border every day, to Saint Eugene's in Derry. I liked school, but not the milk. It had a funny taste. We were given a small bottle of it every day, and a straw to drink it with. Maybe I was used to fresh cows' milk. It was there in Carrigans on the train platform that I learnt to ride a bike. On my way back from school to catch the bus I did a lot of exploring of the city and found that I could walk around the Derry walls to get to the bus station. Whilst I lived with my grandmother I got well used to Derry and always liked to watch the bonfires on the 12th of July. At this time, there was rationing in the South, and you were only allowed so much bread and butter. My grandmother would give me money to buy a loaf in Derry, and I would bring it back over the border under my school bag. The Customs people would take it if they found it. They never did.

On my travels in Donegal and Northern Ireland, flax was all

over the place. It was used for linen making. Now linen is not to be found. The smell was dreadful and you had to put your hand over your mouth.

During my time in Carrigans, a first cousin of my Mam's, Fr Joe Hanahoe, was home on holiday from Tasmania. He said mass in his brother Tommy's house. He asked me to serve mass for him, which I did, but wonder now how did I know what to do, as mass then was said in Latin. Going back to Father Joe, in later life, he became seriously ill while abroad and was sent to England for treatment. Tim and myself met him at Heathrow. Arrangements were already made to which hospital he was to be admitted. He had all the details. We accompanied him to the hospital. He got treated and was sent back to Dublin to his mother Cassie and family. He remained in Dublin for some years and died there at a great age.

While I was with my grandmother, we visited Uncle Joe Gormley, her son, who owned the Ture Inn. She got a bungalow built next to him, towards the end of her life. In later years on our Irish visits, Tim and I went to see Uncle Joe's wife, Aunt Essie who died in a nursing home in Trim, County Meath. Back to Uncle Joe! Uncle Joe took us on lots of trips. One trip was to visit a submarine, and we were able to go inside it. I would have been eleven at the time. The internet fills out the details for me: on 14 May 1945 the first eight German U-boats entered Lough Foyle after they were all given the order to surrender. Around forty to sixty U-boats entered the port of Lisahally and some were brought to Derry where locals could go on board, to look up the periscopes, see the berths and view the torpedo bays. Eventually up to one hundred and fifty submarines were sunk off Malin Head, north Donegal in Operation Deadlight

(20).

As a child I remember my grandmother receiving letters with cheques in from Newcastle, where we now know she had property, referred to in family lore as 'rows of terrace houses'. When she died, my parents told me she had left me £100. I never got it, and all her money went to the White Fathers (21).

Sacred Heart Convent School, Ballyshannon

I returned home in 1947 to go to secondary school in Ballyshannon with Terri, my sister. This was a new secondary department, developed from the Primary school, with Mother Frances McHugh as its first Principal. They were of the order of Sisters of Mercy. At that time, we were all living in Stracomer House and it was too far to travel to Ballyshannon each day. Mam and Dad rented a house in Edenville, north of Kinlough, from Barney Clancy (now 'Spring a Ring', the local taxi service). It was a small house, so they managed to find lodgings for Terri and I in Ballyshannon with Mrs McSherry. Mrs McSherry was somehow related to the original Owen's of Aughavohill. The lodgings were ok and we went to school from there, going home at weekends. Dad bought us by pony and trap down the Moy Road and it was very dangerous in ice and snow. I remember the pony sliding all over the road and then Dad made that journey back on his own- he was a great Dad and passed away when we were all in good positions.

Lovely Nuns

If you got wet on your way to school your coats were taken off and dried for you. Mother Frances had a great love of the country children; she probably came from the country. In the morning if the weather was bad and snow was on the mountains the nuns always spoke about it. We had a lot of homework to do. Terri always wanted to get more marks than me. Mam and Dad had to buy all the books and as we were in the same class, we had to have our own books: poems, history, geography, arithmetic and many more. They were heavy to carry. Anyway, we got there. I remember Margaret G, a 'townie', whilst we were very 'green', coming in from the country. She was wild, and would go to the top of the stairs and drop her heavy school bag right down the stair well. It was amazing she did not kill any of the nuns. She used to tell us lots of tales about boys, but we didn't believe her.

At Ballyshannon School we had the day off when it was Fair Day in the town, as one day a child got killed by an animal at the Fair. That was years earlier than our day. Also, if a nun died, we got the day off.

During my school days in Ballyshannon at lunchtime a group of us went to the bridge to see what was going on. It was the cementation for the hydroelectric power station on the River Erne. Some girls in my class were from England as their fathers were engineers working on it. There was a lot of blasting to erect the "Cathleen's Falls". You may have seen the carved stone memorial to poet William Allingham now on the bridge. We could see lots of dead salmon in the river due to the blasting. We were told often that we were not allowed to go down the town.

Irish and Nuns Re-visited

I hadn't learnt Irish, being away in Derry, and all subjects were taught through the medium of Irish. I was told fifty years later by a nun I didn't have to do Irish! I somehow got my exams in Ballyshannon School and have my certificates.

When I was a student nurse in England, I always went to see the nuns who had taught me, when going home on a visit. Mother Frances would march me up before all the class and say, "Now you all see how 'Maura' did at school- she was a hard worker -take a lesson from how she did!" She would call in the other nuns too to see me. Some years ago, we received a letter that there was a function in the hotel for all pupils from the first year of the Sacred Heart School. I went and we were all presented with a lovely medal. At that stage Terri had died. I should have been given a medal for her family.

Other girls in Ireland had a different experience: if you became pregnant locally and were not married, you were sent to Castlepollard (22); it was run by the Congregation of the Sacred Hearts of Jesus and Mary nuns. This was a great disgrace on the girl's family; maybe those girls stayed there as the parents were ashamed to have them back to their homes. If people asked, "where is your daughter?" "Oh, she is in England and has a great job", they were told. By all accounts these girls were not treated very well by the nuns. Castle Pollard was the place for the north-west; all counties had their own place. The babies as far as I know were adopted. There was a film made of such places called *The Magdalen Sisters.*

Ballyshannon School Exams Certificate June 1949

Intermediate Examination Certificate 1950

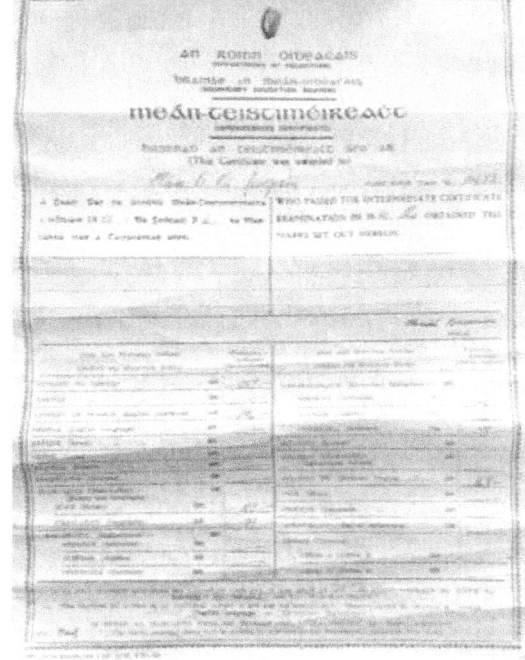

5 EARLY DAYS IN NURSING

First Stop, Back to Derry

I always wanted to do nursing. My Mam asked me to write a letter saying why. I wrote that I liked the uniform and I got a big lecture about that! I applied, got accepted and started to do nurse training in the City and County Hospital in Derry. I was also accepted in Dublin at The Mater Hospital, and St Vincent's, but my parents could not afford the fees. It was difficult to get in to the hospital in Derry, as I was Roman Catholic. Uncle Joe signed some documents and I got in, despite my religion. I do remember that Aunt Essie, Uncle Joe's wife, was very nice when I called to the Ture Inn, when I was a student nurse in Derry. I was not very happy this time round, though I got to know a lot of people and had a boyfriend called Leo Love. I joined a club in the Strand and played a lot of games-hockey, camogie, tennis, but was not much at any of them. As a Roman Catholic, I was given a lot of nasty remarks at work. I was there about six months. and was going to carry on there as it was only due to my Uncle Joe signing those documents that I got in. I was on down on holiday with Mam and Dad and all the family, when out walking I met Kathleen Connolly who was also on holiday from England, where she was doing her nurse training. She asked me about Derry. I told her that I was unhappy there and what I had to do there. She said, "Maureen, write to England". Mam and Dad were not very happy that I was leaving Derry and that I was not going to do nurse training there. During this time, I wrote to England and all the hospitals I applied to accepted me. They always wanted Irish nurses. I had a good selection of hospitals: in Liverpool, Manchester, and Oldchurch Hospital in Romford. I don't know why I accepted Oldchurch, as I didn't know anybody there or in England, except that it sounded good. I came to England in October 1953 coming over on the cattle boat. Where cars are now, that was full of animals. I arrived into Euston Station from Holyhead, but don't remember how I got to Romford. Mam always said be careful who you speak to for directions, such as a policeman, so I will have followed that advice anyway.

Oldchurch Hospital

It was my first Christmas away from home, and I remember being on a male medical ward. The staff were very nice to me, and the patients knew that it was my first Christmas away. The patients were forever asking me to speak and one man tried to imitate my Irish accent. Later there was a male patient who kept asking me to say the word 'thunder'. I suppose there was thunder in the weather (23). I have photos of those days at Oldchurch. After arriving in October 1953, Preliminary Training School (PTS) commenced in December 1953.

At Oldchurch Hospital in 1953 you had to take patients to the bathroom on your own and lift heavy patients in and out of the bath. There was no help and you had to do this. Years later special lifting aids were brought in: years too late for me and others– myself, I developed a bad back. This is common to nurses. The nurses of today are shown how to do all sorts of things: ECGs, taking blood, scans. I found this out when I was a patient in a Northern General Hospital in Sheffield and also as a patient in Queens and King Georges Hospital, Essex.

On arrival, you were allocated a bedroom and bathroom in the Nurses Home, and it was very comfortable. There were about eighty to one hundred in my (PTS). I soon got to know a lot of them, and up to a few years ago I was in contact with many friends. All were Irish, Welsh or Scottish. We had an intense training: very hard. It will always stand by me.

As a student you had to do a lot of night duties. One night when I was maybe in my second year I was in charge of a large medical ward when the night superintendent came to do her round. It was your duty to go around with her to each patient and tell her about each patient. I remember I did know all about each one. She arrived and well I remember seeing her beside me: I was sitting in the middle of the ward. I was unable to get up, and she had to do the round on her own. Miss Tavener was her name. I was very upset; I thought I would get a bad mark and have to go to the Matron in the morning. I did not have to, and I was told the following night that I had 'night nurse's cramp', maybe by Miss Tavener. I had never heard of this before; some of the nurses did know about it, but they never had the experience that I had.

My first pay was £8 a month, but you didn't have to spend any as all was included – bed and board. I sent money to Mam and Dad, but it was returned to me by them. I bought a big wrist watch which I was very proud of- where did it end up? - as you could not wear jewellery, only a wedding ring in those days. There was a lot more that I can remember: Breakfast 8am, not much dinner 1pm, with custard on all desserts. The Welsh girl in my PTS she fell out of her seat in a lecture onto the floor! She also came to Goodmayes Hospital.

Oldchurch Hospital First Christmas. Maureen right

Oldchurch Hospital First Christmas. Maureen right

With Eric Who Wanted Me to Say 'Thunder'

Studying and Time Off

The training was excellent. I used to go and lie in the bath to study. During PTS we had exams every week. How we passed, I don't know, as we always went out to dances, including at Saint Peters Church in Dagenham. There were no electric lights in the hall, so there were gas lights at that time. We travelled there and back by bus. We had to be in at 10:30pm unless you got a late pass. If you mentioned the Shandon Dance Hall in Romford, the matron Miss Hooley from Sligo would say "No late pass" (24). We all enjoyed the Shandon and watched out for new blokes arriving. We put nicknames on them: one very good-looking lad who had his collar in tatters -we called him "shirt from Mullingar". There were no drinks served- only orange juice, but the men would come in half full of alcohol. "Keep your distance from them", we were told. One of my friends from Spiddal in

Galway had a room on the bottom floor of the Nurses Home. She would leave her window open so we could all get in and run as fast as we could to our rooms. I can still hear the noise of the taffeta, which was all the fashion in those days!

Then we heard about The Blarney in Tottenham Court Road (25) and were off there for 3pm on Sundays. We didn't have money to go to the dance as well as pay for the train, so we got platform tickets. At Tottenham Court Road you were asked, "Where did you get on?" We all said the station before Tottenham Court Road. I'm sure the ticket collector knew. You could not do that now. Once or twice, we got to Liverpool Street and went to the police station and asked them to take us back to Romford, and they did take us back. The next time we went to the police station we were told to go back and wait for the next train!

During your training, I suppose in your second year, you got a blue belt. If you were caught coming in late you had to go to Matron's Office -which was always is a big thing anyway, and it meant you lost your blue belt. Everyone knew why you lost your belt. If we had to come in the proper way and be checked in at the door, some of the women were nice and didn't book us.

Of all the wards, only the Eye Ward was not nice, because of the Ward Sister. She always said, "No noise whatsoever". All patients were only cataract operations. It is strange as now this operation is day only. I enjoyed all other ward training, which was excellent.

In Oldchurch Hospital there was a unit which we were not allowed to go into. I think it was called Waterloo House. We did ask, "why not?" but we were not told during our training. The patients there were not called by their names, and were only known by numbers. They were all suffering from gonorrhoea which is a sexually transmitted disease. I think that it was eventually closed, with new treatments being brought in.

I must say I enjoyed my training; it was good and will be in my mind always. I got my State Registered Nurse qualification (SRN) March 1957, first go and was very proud. I was accepted for Midwifery at Oldchurch Hospital. My friend Ruth and I decided to live out. You had to notify Matron's Office and she would go and inspect the premises. You had to produce a letter from your parents saying it was okay for you to live out. We always got someone else to write the letter! I don't know if Matron ever went to inspect the place, but the letter must have passed her scrutiny.

Oldchurch Hospital Christmas Nativity.
Maureen back row far left

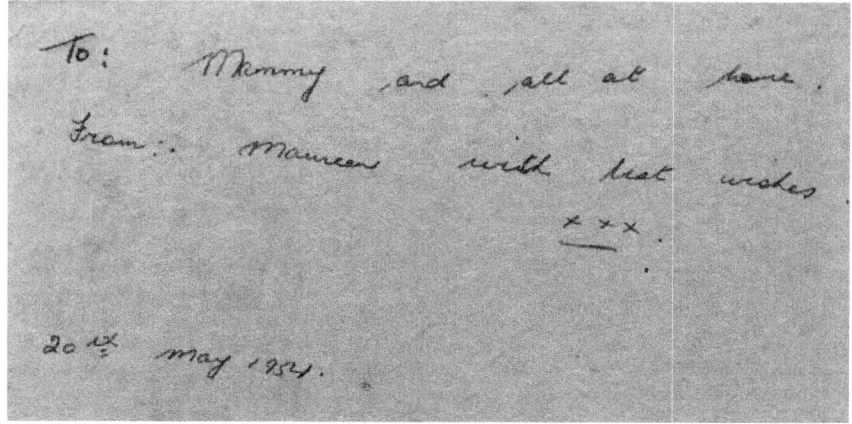

To: Mummy and all at home.
From:. Maureen with best wishes.
x x x.

20th May 1954.

**Oldchurch Hospital 2nd Year Block July 1956.
Maureen front row 3rd from left**

Maureen on left with nursing student friends 1956

Oldchurch Hospital Staff Nurse

HOSPITAL MANAGEMENT COMMITTEE
(ROMFORD GROUP)

OLDCHURCH HOSPITAL

ROMFORD

Certificate

awarded to

Mary B. Fergus

who has trained in this Hospital for a period of 3 years from 5th Dec 1953 to 5th Dec 1956.

She has received tuition and had practical experience on the wards in accordance with the Syllabus of the General Nursing Council for England and Wales, and has passed the Hospital Examination.

Dated this Eighteenth day of March 1957

Examiner

Examiner

Examiner

Matron

Medical Superintendent

Chairman of the Hospital Management Committee

SRN Qualification Oldchurch Hospital 1957

Romance at The Blarney

As I said, I was to start Midwifery and, in the meantime, I met Tipperary Tim at the Blarney, a wonderful choice. I was dancing with someone else and Tim said "keep the next dance for me", which I did and he asked if he could meet me the next weekend. I also had a date with another lad the same night. I kept the date with Tim! I told my brothers, Hugh and Aidan, who were then working in London, that I had met Tim and was meeting him again. The next week they both came to see this bloke I was meeting, and they approved. Tim was working in a pub in Stratford and told me he had applied to Goodmayes Hospital to do nurse training (Psychiatric), so I didn't take up Midwifery. Instead, I also applied to Goodmayes Hospital.

My blue taffeta dress

**Siblings in London in the 50s.
Left to right Terri, Hugh, Maureen, Aiden**

Goodmayes Hospital

The hospital had opened as West Ham Borough Asylum in 1901; became the West Ham Mental Hospital in 1918, and joined the NHS as Goodmayes Hospital in 1948. Tim had been a patient in the Isolation Hospital (later, Chadwell Heath Hospital) with measles I think and was being nursed by a staff nurse whose husband worked at Goodmayes Hospital. He came to visit his wife and spoke to Tim: that is why he went to Goodmayes Hospital to work. In 1957 when I started by training, there were 1,331 patients.

Nurses with their SRN transferring to Goodmayes were not accepted by the staff. If they knew you had SRN they were heard to say "WHAT- ANOTHER BLOODY SRN". Maybe it was because we only had to do one and a half years and the nurses doing their initial training there had to do three years. I had to give one month's notice at Oldchurch Hospital, and was refused three or four times. Then I found out who was in the office, waiting for a sympathetic recipient, so then gave in my notice. I did my Registered Mental Nurse training (RMN), and qualified in April 1959. Dad had to do three years. He got his qualification-he was bright and studied. He had to go to Claybury Hospital for part of his PTS. He had a bike so it was a good way to travel for him. With Tim there before me, I suppose it was good for my acceptance by staff, as he had said I would be joining him.

There was an underground passage below the entire hospital. The entrance was in the grounds; we being curious did go down into it. Maybe it was used during the war for safety for patients, as that area was at risk of bombing during the War.

In the grounds there was a lovely church, seating 600 people, and staff took patients to Sunday services. I remember a baby being christened in the church. I never went into the church as we were told by our parents it was a sin to do so as we were Roman Catholic. The church was eventually demolished for a car park.

Young Nurses

No men were allowed to go to your room in the Nurses Home, which was on site. A lot were 'got' (caught breaking the rules) and I don't know what happened to them.

When I was a student, many nurses came from London hospitals to do their training in psychiatry. There was a group of male nurses watching out for them coming and they would pick a few nurses that they fancied. You would hear them saying, "She looks okay!" It was "take your pick!" One chap was Paddy from Sligo and another was Ewing. In fact, one Goodmayes male nurse did marry a London hospital nurse and is now living in Romford with a grown-up family and grandchildren; I'm in touch with them. I don't remember the rest of that gang. I think Paddy went to work on an ocean liner.

In Goodmayes whilst training as an SRN, I did come across some very sad cases. We were all given MF keys, which opened all doors. Most of the wards were locked at first, but soon most were opened, except on the wards for patients with dementia. A special lock was put up higher on the doors to avoid them getting out and getting lost. On one Admission Ward there was a padded room. This room was padded from floor to the roof and patients who were in this room had special clothes on them which they could not rip. They were on constant watch and when medication was given, you were accompanied by other nurses, maybe three nurses depending on the state of the patient. We had only one padded room in those days. We could have had more such rooms. One day a student nurse felt sorry for the patient in the padded room, and let her out. Sometime later that nurse was at Mass and caused a disturbance with the priest. She eventually was admitted to Claybury Hospital (psychiatric). There was also, I believe, a padded room on one of the male wards, but I don't know which ward.

Goodmayes Hospital Tennis Club

Goodmayes Hospital panto. Tim Ryan, student nurse on right

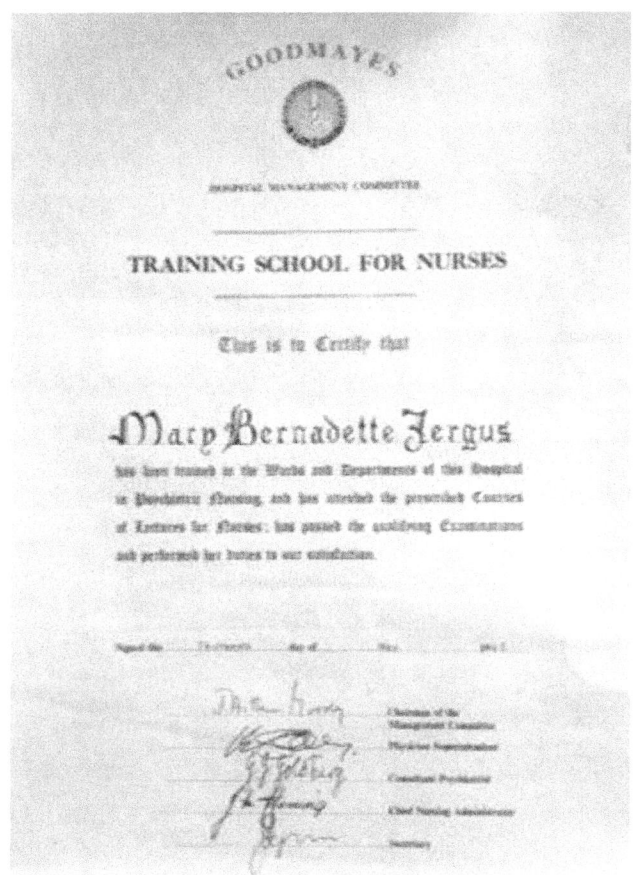

RMN Nursing Qualification Goodmayes Hospital

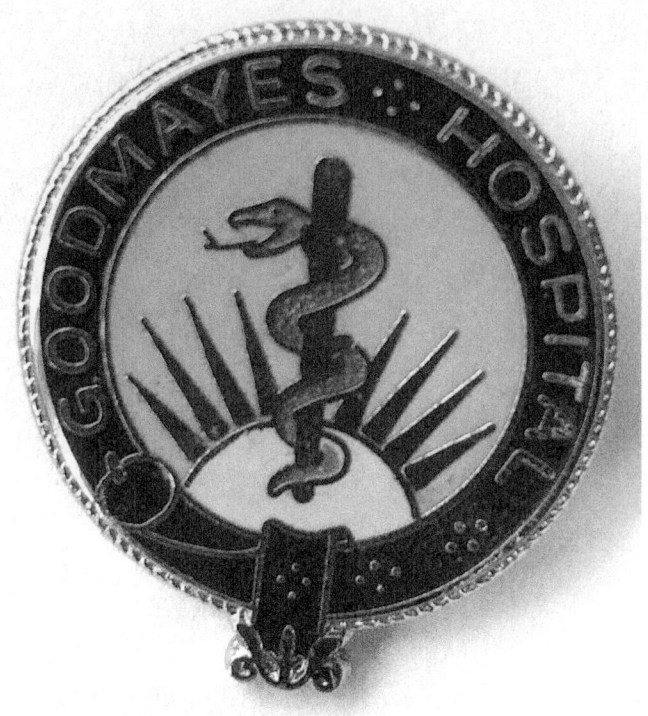

SRN badge with RMN qualification added

6 WEDDING BELLS

We got married on 31st of March 1959 at Saint Peter and Paul's Catholic Church in Ilford, by Father Duckett. I think you got a tax rebate if you married before the end of the year- Tim knew about that. Our Reception was in the Cauliflower Pub (26), near Seven Kings Station. It was a big wedding, with a lot from Ireland coming over. We looked for a flat - in those days in shop windows all advertisements for flats said "No Irish, no Blacks need apply". I think we were recommended for our flat at 62, Norfolk Road. I was already living on Norfolk Road with Marian Callinan and I was gathering all the stuff for my 'bottom drawer'. Marian was not very pleased, as it was a small flat. My Mam and Dad came over for our wedding and stayed with Tim at 62 Norfolk Road.

On my way to the altar Dad kept standing on my dress. It was his first time to England, and last, as he got leukaemia for which the only treatment then was blood transfusion. Going home on holiday while I was a student I remember the train to Holyhead, boat to Dublin, then train to Sligo, to be always met by my Dad. I well remember Tim and myself going home before Katharine was born, being met by Hugh, my brother, and him saying Dad was in hospital. I remember when Katharine was two and went into the hospital to visit him. He adored Katharine, his first grandchild, and thought the world of Tim Ryan. He died in the Sheil Hospital, Ballyshannon on 3rd September 1963.

Our Wedding Day 31 March 1959

Gertie's Wedding 1961, Left to Right Cathal, Maureen, Jim McHugh, Gertie, Mam, Pat, Hugh, Aiden. Terri was in America.

7 NURSING LIFE, FAMILY LIFE, PAY AND PROMOTION

The Irish Family

Goodmayes Hospital was very family orientated. If anybody was in difficulties, or the father or mother had died in Ireland, we collected the fare for them to go to Ireland. We all got married around the same time; a lot from Goodmayes were at our wedding and up to now I keep very much in contact with many people from there.

Dinner dances at Goodmayes were a big event. We all wore long expensive dresses and all the big noises from the hospital were there so we were all on our best behaviour. One of the matrons, Mrs Herrick, ordered a special dress for a dance. One of the nurses, Ethel Kennedy (RIP), managed to get the dress from the post, and wore it to the dance. Mrs Herrick never got to know what happened to her dress. Ethel eventually married a doctor; I often wonder how she got on; I think she came from Cork.

At Goodmayes nearly all nurses were Irish. Our matron for

years was Mrs Herring, a lovely person; her parents were McGoldrick, again from Cork; she was kind to all of us. She told me one day that another Fergus was coming -Ann Fergus from Loughrea, County Galway, but no relation to me.

New Parents and Nursing

We lived in our flat in Norfolk Road for two years. It was very nice, but I was then expecting our wonderful girl and we needed a house. We went to the estate agent and said to put it in joint names as we were both working. Dad had money saved and we saved a lot. We liked Gresham Drive and bought it for £3000. Katharine was born on the 9th of February 1961 at 9 o'clock: 6 lb 12 oz. After having a baby, at that time mams had to go back to work six weeks later; not like now when they get one year, and husbands get time off also.

As a baby Katharine and many more children of staff were cared for by Mrs Frost. She is now aged 93. Katharine called her 'Mammy Frost'. Tim and I did opposite shifts, early and late -7am until 2pm, and 2pm until 9pm. I well remember one day Katharine was dressed in a nice furry coat. The snow was heavy and as I wheeled her over the road to Mrs Frost, she fell out of the pram into the snow. She thought it was great fun -not me- I was very worried. She was always strapped in properly after that.

Danny and Eileen were close family friends from these early days, as Eileen was a nurse in Goodmayes too. Their eldest son Barry is six months older than Katharine and was also looked after by 'Mammy Frost'. There was a sweet shop at the end of Barley Lane in Goodmayes and Barry told the owner he was going to marry Katharine. The owner apparently said to Eileen, "I wonder if they will".

After Tim got his RMN, he left Goodmayes Hospital to work in Fords in Dagenham. The Ilford Pictorial, the local newspaper, found out he was leaving nursing - how, I don't know. They arrived at the door, and though he was cross at the time, he was proud of the big article entitled, "Why I Resigned – by a Nurse". His decision was quoted in Parliament by Laurie Pavitt, M.P., March 1962 as evidence of the crisis in hospitals caused by low pay and poor working conditions. Tim is quoted as saying, "At present it isn't a living wage for a man with a home and family to keep".

When we went to Gresham Drive there was no church and separate school -the school and church were all one building. The priest there asked all parishioners to give £25 for a stone to build a new school and church- all done! Our mortgage in Gresham Drive was £15.28 a month. Sometimes it proved difficult, but with dad at Fords it became easy.

I used to take Katharine in the bike seat down to Gertie, my sister and family. They lived in Mortlake Road, Ilford. I cycled over Gresham Drive, down Barley Lane past the hospital to Seven Kings. We got there safe, but when I think of it now, it was very dangerous, though traffic was not as it is now.

When Katharine was growing up, she got a lot of presents from us, from neighbours and relatives. I don't think she ever wrote to Father Christmas; maybe she did. The things that we brought for her were left with Irene and Cliff, our neighbours next door. When she was asleep on Christmas Eve, we collected them all. She actually said one year, "I got a lot of presents from a lot of people, and Fr Christmas, but none from you!" There were Christmas parties held nearby in Somerville Hall for the children. Tim sometimes was Father Christmas; I think Katharine may have recognised him on one occasion.

New parents Gresham Drive

Gresham Drive

At home in Gresham Drive

WHY I RESIGNED —BY A NURSE

THE man who loved nursing—but gave the job u because of the low pay, told the Pictorial this week "I was doing a worthwhile job at the hospital. But have to think of my family."

Timothy Ryan's decision earned him mention in Parliament last week, when Labour M.P. Laurie Pavitt quoted his case as typical of the crisis in our hospitals with experienced nurses leaving because of poor pay and conditions.

A quiet-voiced, 32-year-old Irishman, Mr. Ryan talked about his decision this week in his brightly-decorated, new home in Gresham Drive—only a short walk away from Goodmayes Hospital where he worked for five years. A few weeks ago he resigned, and now works at Ford's, where he earns a minimum of £16 a week as a grinder.

Overtime

"My average take-home pay was around £10, after five years there, including three years being trained for the job. Doing 10 hours or so in overtime brought it up to about £13.

"Then in January the Ministry ended paid overtime. That meant I could be asked to work a 64-hour week with no chance of increasing my basic pay. All we can get for overtime now is time off—when the hospital can spare us."

It was the ending of paid overtime that made Mr. Ryan decide—reluctantly—that he could not afford to stay in nursing.

It would have taken another four years, he pointed out, for him to earn the top staff nurse rate. And even that is below £14.

Then there are the long hours, working at nights and weekends, and the responsibilities of being left alone in charge of a large ward when there are not enough charge nurses to go round.

"But you don't get any extra money for taking charge of a ward, unless you do it for 13 weeks of a year. You can do a charge nurse's job for 12 weeks and get no compense."

Mr. Ryan said he thought that even if the Ministry agreed to a big pay rise no

might not help the staff short age immediately. Not all th trained nurses who had lef would return to the hospital and if more student nurse came in they would not b trained for another three year:

"I would probably go back i there was a reasonable pa rise," he said. "At present, i isn't a living wage for a mar with a home and family t keep."

Essential

Mr. Ryan started to buy hi home on mortgage last year Playing with blonde, 14-month old baby Katherine, he said "Nursing is an essential servic to the community. But wher the mortgage payments ar due and the bills come in, can't tell the people they wil have to go without their money because I am a nurse."

The Deputy Head Male Nurse at Goodmayes, Mr. Joseph Soley, this week described Mr. Ryan as, "One of our best prospects. His work was excellent, and his leaving us is a real loss."

And Mr. Pavitt told the House of Commons, "He had a natural flair for mental nursing—which is not one of the easiest tasks—and his ward reports were excellent."

March 1962

Things Keep Popping into my Head

I had a bike with a seat on it, that Katharine used to ride in. There was a patient who apparently felt sorry for me with having the baby and also working. One night I went to collect my bike to go home and my basket was full of groceries. If I was stopped by Security, I would have got the sack. The patient's name was Alice. I spoke to Alice and asked her not to do that again. After that incident I always checked my carrier: in fact, she did do the same again, but luckily, I sorted it out.

If any plants got too big for our house in Gresham Drive, we would take them over to the hospital, and give them to a ward. At home Katharine had a budgie and when she lost interest in it, off he went to Goodmayes to one of the wards. I remember one lady called May. One day she said to me, "Sister Ryan, that budgie talks Irish" It could have had, as I was not very good at Irish.

Nurses Pay

The issue of low wages which had led to Tim leaving nursing in 1962, remained unresolved, and in 1974 we went on strike. My great friend Betty reminded me of the details. Union leaders visited the wards to check there was enough staffing to keep the patients safe and give them their dinner. We then left the wards and went by coaches to gather at a park in Romford for a rally. On another day we walked out and went on coaches to Ilford where we walked along the High Road in uniform. We demonstrated outside the House of Commons, and there was a rally in Hyde Park. We wanted to see Keith Joseph, but Barbara Castle came out to meet us instead. The nurses' action led to an independent inquiry and overall pay increases averaging 30%.

By 1982, low pay was again an issue for nurses and other NHS workers and we campaigned for a 12% pay rise. On Wednesday 22 September over two million people took part in strike action, including supportive action by car workers at Fords and Vauxhall, with over 80% of mines closed, and the Post Office. We all went into the big hall in Goodmayes. Mrs Herring was not very happy about it. We went and stood outside the gates, and there is a photo of us with placards. I remember of friend ours, John Joyce saying, "we at Fords went out in sympathy with you" (more of the Joyces later). The Government improved their offer to 12.3% over two years and set up an Independent Pay Review Body.

Nurses on strike 1974, Betty right, Maureen left

Nurses Strike Meeting Goodmayes Hospital

Ward Sister and Nursing Officer

After my RMN, some years on I became Sister in Charge. Whilst I was a Ward Sister, I was asked by the Matron, Mrs Herring if I could arrange to open a mother and baby unit on Gregory Ward, which I did. It turned out to be a great success. All baby equipment was supplied by the hospital until we had an episode where husbands were taking home the baby things. It was then decided that everything would be supplied by the family.

Chest Clinic was one of many of my duties. Dr A. came from Ilford Chest Clinic, and he smoked continuously during the Clinic. He saw to the staff for the BCG vaccination (27), as well as patients. There was one male patient who knew when Dr A. was there and somehow found out about his smoking habit. He would wait outside the Clinic for the remnants of his cigarettes. Katharine as a child was due to have the BCG at school. I got upset that she was going to be injected when I wasn't there. I told Dr A. and he asked me to bring Katharine to see him and he did the vaccination at the Ilford Chest Clinic.

As a Ward Sister I was in charge of the ECT unit, as well as the Chest Clinic, Dental and Optical clinics, and Staff Health. How I coped, I often wonder. When new gadgets came in, I had to instruct the staff how to use them e.g., water beds, ripple beds. I did the Family Planning Certificate at Saint Paul's in London, when I was Occupational Health Officer. Then a post came up for Nursing Officer, so I applied and got it: the position I held until retirement in 1987. I had a wonderful retirement party with lots of presents.

Katharine came this morning (Monday 1st June 2020), and brought my shopping. She has been reading *The History of Goodmayes Hospital 1886-1989*. It makes for fascinating reading, particularly the details about the early patients admitted,

"Some of the women who were admitted were pregnant, and any child born in the hospital was also certified as 'insane' and kept there- often for the rest of their lives. The last 'patient' who was admitted here because they were born on the premises only died a few years ago." (28)

I do remember this person, who despite later efforts to move her to the community, knew no other world and would not go. This leads me to more things that I had forgotten. Goodmayes had a lot of amenities for the patients such as chiropody, a hairdresser, beauty therapy. These were not for staff! There was an Operating Theatre, and a range of operations were carried out there, such as leucotomies (cutting some of the nerve fibres in the frontal lobe of the brain). I did see this operation performed by special visiting surgeons. Dental and optical treatments were carried out by outside specialists. There was a shop for patients and staff, selling cigarettes, sweets etc. A dress shop was also there. There was a lovely Occupational Therapy unit, and in the 1950s all student nurses had to do a placement there. While I was there, I made a stool, and a teddy for Katharine from red furry material. I think she still has it.

Just picked up this information from the Internet: Sir Ian Holm, actor, died today the 19th of June 2020. He was born in Goodmayes Hospital on 12th of September 1931 where his father was a psychiatrist and his mother was a nurse. His parents probably lived in hospital accommodation. His father was a pioneer of electric shock treatment, introducing ECT to Goodmayes Hospital.

Celebration in Main Hall at Goodmayes. Maureen second right

Goodmayes Hospital Ward Sister back right, including nurses from The London Hospital

Goodmayes Hospital Nursing Officer ECT Department, Maureen centre

Goodmayes Hospital OT Department 1958. Maureen making a stool, in full uniform

Red teddy

Legacy

While I was at Goodmayes, I asked if they could provide a Creche. I got names of staff in all grades at the hospital who supported it -nurses, doctors, cleaners, but was not granted this project. When I was retired, years after, the Creche was built. I got an invitation to go to the opening. I didn't go-why, I don't know. The invite was from Paul Gokie, so my idea must have still been on record.

Volunteering

After retirement I worked as a volunteer in the hospice for some years; then in the local MS (Multiple Sclerosis) unit and in the SENSE charity shop. The MS unit was a very interesting place. All I did there was to make tea, talk to the clients and help in the kitchen. They were all given a nice cooked meal, all done by voluntary workers. I also worked in Vincent's Charity Shop in Bundoran, Ireland during our visits there, so I kept busy.

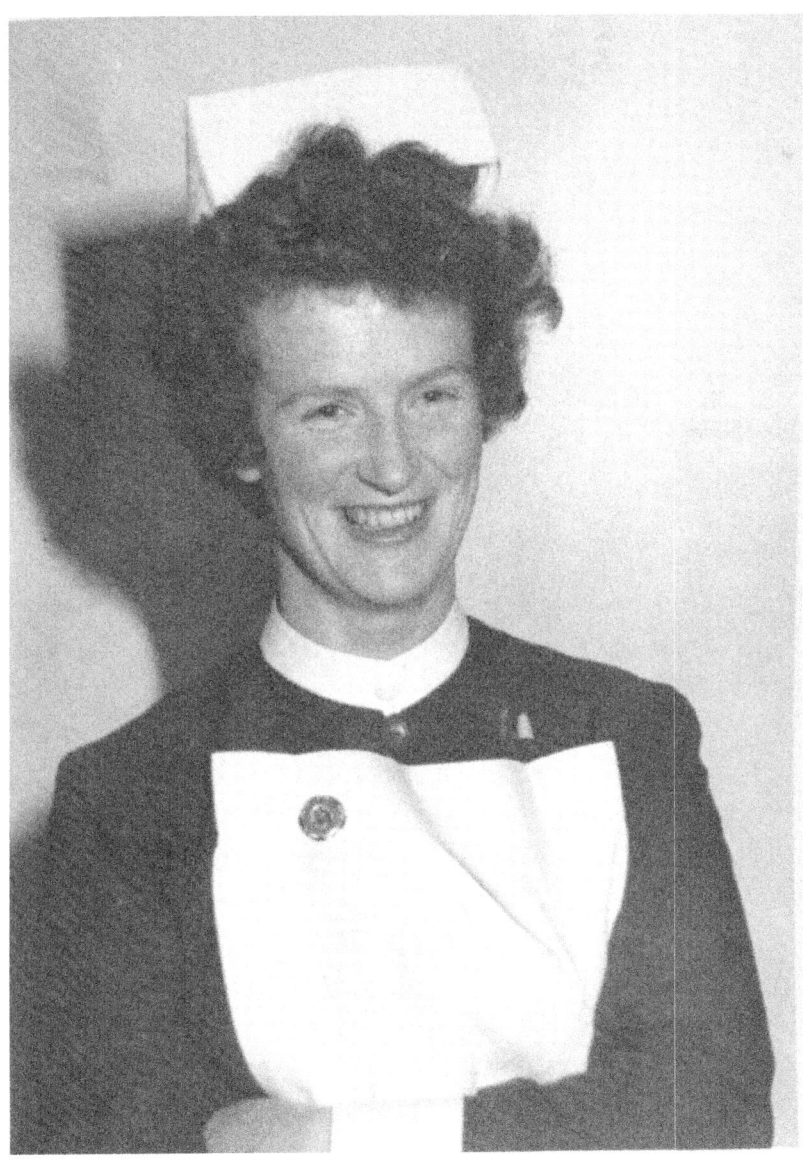

8 BACK TO SCHOOL DAYS AND FAST FORWARD BEYOND

As Katharine grew up and went to Saint Bede's Primary School, Mrs Cox then collected her from school if I was working. She made friends at Saint Bede's and I got to know all the mams. After that she did the Entrance Exam and went to the Ursuline High School in Ilford. If you lived more than 3 miles away you could get a free bus pass, so we drove the bus route and got free travel for her after we had been turned down.

Learning to Drive
Katharine entered a competition when she was about 15, and one of the prizes was driving lessons. We were unaware of this until one night a man came to the door to say she had won a number of free lessons. We laughed, saying she was only 15, then she said to me, "you could do the lessons", so I did! I think his name was Murphy. I had those lessons and then got lessons from BSM. Dad took me over to the car drome in Hornchurch, an old airfield for practice. One day our friend John Joyce, took me out for a drive. We arrived back okay. Dad said, "how was it, Joycie?" "Ryan, give me a

double brandy quick! That woman nearly killed me!" he replied. I passed first time, as I think the Test Examiner took pity on me. I went wearing my full nursing sister uniform.

Off to The Palace

While Katharine was at the Ursuline, she gained the Duke of Edinburgh Award. The Gold Award was presented by the Duke of Edinburgh in Buckingham Palace. Tim and I were very proud of Katharine getting this. Only one parent could go in to the Palace, so dad asked me to go. We had a photo taken in Buckingham Palace. You were not allowed to take your own photos in there and cameras were taken off you. It was a great day. Dad was allowed to park on Pall Mall, the road opposite the Palace.

From the Ursuline she got a place at The University of Sheffield and did very well. She met 'Everton Tim', a wonderful choice. We first met him in a hospital in Sheffield when he was visiting Katharine after she had her appendix out! They got married at Saint Edward's Church in Romford on the 18th of August 1984, a great day. As a young nurse at Oldchurch Hospital, this was the first church in England that I went to. A special card came from the Everton Football Team. Paul, Tim's brother knew and at the end of his Best Man's speech and having read out a few cards, he produced this card. Tim's friends didn't believe it was real at first. All Katharine's aunts and uncles on both sides who were able, attended the wedding.

9 DEAR OLD FRIENDS

Now I have mentioned the Joyce family before now. Tim met John whilst working at Fords. John Joyce had an accident and dad went to see him at home. I said, "Did you meet his wife?" and dad replied, "She was in the kitchen all the time!" They and we all became great friends, with their children around the same age as Katharine. Their friendship and kindness were so practical too: after meeting them, all decorating in Gresham Drive was done with the help of John, Alice and Danny. Dad as far as I remember, did not assist decorating at the Joyce residence!

You may remember, or have heard of Sister John Maria. One year on holiday in Tipperary, Tim and I went to visit Peg Kennedy (Harrington). She was talking to dad about her sister, a nun, Sr. John who was teaching in Liverpool. She had been told by her seniors that she was being transferred to Chigwell, Essex. Sister John was very upset. Dad said, "that is only up the way from where we are". This is what started a great time for all. She was made Headteacher of a school for children with special needs in Chigwell. As Headteacher, she organised a summer fayre each year to raise money for the school. It involved Tim, Danny and John and many more friends going up there to set out the stalls the night before, then running the Bottle Stall....!. It turned out a great success every year. The night before the event Sr John would put out the statue of the 'Child of Prague' to ward off the rain (29). Well, Surprise it worked! - every year! Katharine as a teenager always joined in; also, Alice, Eileen, and many more. (I often wondered is that where Katharine got to know what she wanted to do in her life?) If so, Katharine, dad and I were very proud of you, all your studies, and what you and Tim obtained, and your two wonderful sons- God bless.

Our regular socialising was at Saint Edward's Catholic Club, Romford, my first church as a young nurse at Oldchurch. One night after the Club, a group of our friends, including Danny and John Mc came back to our house and took the plastic deer head we had up on the wall in the hall. Danny kept it and we never missed it. Sister John Maria then had a raffle up at Chigwell at the school. We bought a lot of tickets and of course, we had the winning ticket! Guess what it was? - it was the deer head! Tim opened it and said, "We have one like that at home."

Another night we were in Saint Cede's Catholic Club in Goodmayes and as usual back it was to Joyces afterwards. Tim Murray, Tim Ryan and Danny took their garden gate off. They carried it upstairs and placed it nicely in John and Alice's bed! Tim Murray can tell about that event.

While we were in Gresham Drive, there was a family there, the Johnsons, with two sons Chris and Peter. One day I visited them and they were upset as Peter had been made redundant from his job as a teacher. Some hours later, Sr

John came to visit us with another nun. She was in a state as she needed a teacher urgently. "Do you happen to know of a teacher looking for work?" she said. "Yes! Yes Sr John", I said, and went over to the Johnsons and brought Peter back to our house. He was introduced, and after the appropriate procedures, got the job! He was there until he retired. He met his wife too, as I think she was a teacher there. Mr and Mrs Johnson became great friends to Sr John. One Christmas she hired a helicopter and dressed Mr Johnson in a Father Christmas costume to meet the children and deliver presents to them. After retirement Peter and his wife moved up north to be nearer their children, but came down to London for Sr John's funeral. Another teacher at the school in Chigwell got married and had their honeymoon with Cathal and Marlene's house in Ireland.

More memories

Our friends, Maria and Hugh lived near us on Gresham Drive. Maria came over one day and said that Hugh was not very well. Danny and Eileen were in our house at the time, so Danny and Tim Ryan went over, lit candles and went up to Hugh in his bed and were about to start saying prayers. Well, it was a miracle! Hugh jumped out of bed and didn't complain again, to the best of my knowledge.

Lourdes, Customs, and a Small World

Sr John used to go on pilgrimages to Lourdes, taking children from the school. One year Danny and Eileen were also going to help. Marlene, my sister- in- law got a phone call from Sr John telling her that all travel arrangements were made, but she didn't have any idea what she was talking about. Cathal, my brother had put her name down without telling her. She went with them and said it was a marvellous experience interacting with the children. She was very impressed with the way Lourdes was lit up with all the lights, and with the singing of all the hymns. Marlene went in the pool in the Grotto, and was amazed at all the sticks that were left there following cures. Each night ended up with a sing-song. I'm sure Marlene gave a song or two. A man gave her a Miraculous Medal that had been presented to him. She came back with a large bottle of holy water, only to be stopped by the Customs. She got it through, but told me she has none left now. I remember Danny telling us about the holy water: "She has enough for all Bundoran!"

Marlene reminded me of another visit to Lourdes, that I had forgotten about. On my niece Karina's anniversary (daughter of Hugh and Rita), Cathal arranged for Rita and family to go to Lourdes. Marlene said it was a very sad occasion. I do remember Rita telling me about it. There were a lot of groups there, as there is all the time. Rita met a woman from Clarecastle, Co Clare. She spoke to the family, and it turned out it was Ada Power, Tim's niece on pilgrimage in honour of Patrick her brother, who was killed in a car accident coming back from a sick call as a doctor. It's a small world. They also met a couple from nearby Ballyshannon, and still see them from time to time.

Our Lovely Neighbours

When we went to live in Gresham Drive, we were the only Irish people there. We got to know all the residents; then as the years past, people moved or old age came and they died. The houses were bought by new people, and they were all very nice. About 20 years ago a young family who were Muslim moved nearby in Gresham Drive. The children were all very young. We had snow soon after their arrival and they all went out on the grass. They were so excited as it hardly ever snowed properly in London so it was a new experience.

I know Khalilah (30) was born in Luton. Some years after, they were expecting a baby in March. Dad always said to Khalilah the baby would be born on Saint Patrick's Day. Well, Saint Patrick's Day came and went: no baby. On the 19th of March the girls came and told us they had a new sister, Alima. When Tim died in 2006, they came to the house, which was much appreciated. On her way back from work, Khalilah often called for me to come over and have dinner with the family. This was a regular treat. She was my best friend there. In December 2019, I had a phone call inviting Katharine, Tim and myself to Fareeha's wedding, but we were unable to go as it was too close to Christmas and Katharine had invited fourteen friends that day for dinner! There was 500 at the wedding. Since I moved to Sheffield, Khalilah contacts me and keeps me up-to-date with family and local news. Her mum often visited at their house from Luton; sadly, she died in 2020.

10 MY SIBLINGS

Terri, RIP, travelled to many places including America and London. She married and had two boys Aiden and Daniel. She then lived in Dun Laoghaire, before moving to Strandhill, Sligo and eventually Bundoran, where she opened the Equestrian School. **Hugh**, RIP, spent some years in London and returned home to Stracomer to the farm. He married Rita, Principal Teacher in Askill, which is across the lake from Stracomer, where the plane came down. Rita became Principal in Tullaghan, Co Leitrim until her retirement. **Aiden**, RIP, was always a daredevil. He also went to London, working in the Brazen Head Pub in London with Hugh. You will remember me saying Hugh and Aidan came to the Blarney to see 'this boyfriend of mine', who was 'passed okay'. Aidan went back to Ireland, later returning to England, where he married Shirley and lived in Doncaster. After some years they both returned to Bundoran. **Gertie** did commence nursing but did not continue. She got married to Jim McHugh from Sligo, and is now living in Doncaster, a short distance from me. I did go to see her regularly with Katharine, until the virus.

'Cathal' is the Irish for 'Charlie' or 'Charles'. My mother did say that Cathal was called that after my Dad, Charles Joseph Fergus, but she didn't want Cathal to be called Charles. She said, "One Charlie is enough in our house!" I always called him Cathal, but most people call him Charlie. He worked all over, spending most of his life in the UK, and was a big contractor in the building trade. He helped build an oil rig in Kishorn, Scotland, which was opened by Prince Charles (31). Cathal got a coach and went back over to Kinlough, Co. Leitrim as there was not much work there for the local men. He brought a lot of them over to Scotland, and old people there now in Kinlough admire him as it was their sons that built the rig with him. There is a song composed about it, "The Kishorn Commandos", and I have a copy in my special memory box. During this time, he met and married Marlene, (a great day for all). He now lives in Bundoran and has built a lot of houses in Ireland.

Pat, RIP, also commenced nursing but gave it up after a short while. She married Colin Geagan in England; came back to Ireland; lived in Cork and then Bundoran, opening Homefield House Backpackers Hostel. She opened the Language School in nearby premises, and carried on the Equestrian School after the death of Terri.

My brothers and sisters, to me, did well in life. I do like to keep in contact with all their families: nieces and nephews.

11 GATHERING UP THOUGHTS

Hair Colours and Cuts

My mother would never allow her hair to be seen grey. She went to the hairdresser every week in Bundoran. She never went out without an umbrella, gloves and hat. I well remember going to a wedding in Tipperary. My hair was going grey, and she said, "you can't go to a wedding with grey hair". Well, I did go and enjoyed the day! As a child I was blessed with a mop of curly hair. it must've been difficult for my mum to manage it. At school in Ballyshannon all the girls wanted to comb my curls. For years after that I used to go to a hairdresser until one day Tim said, "why go to have your curls cut out?". Then I decided to trim my own hair, until I settled on going to the hairdressers every six weeks, which is what I do now. With the virus I again started to trim my hair. I don't know the reaction my hairdresser will have, as she came here before the virus to cut my hair and the hair of many more of the ladies. It turned out in conversation that Tim Murray taught some of her family- "a small world", as they say.

I may have forgotten to mention Katharine's hair. It was lovely and long- difficult to brush and manage at times. When she was a young child, I remember her grandfather in Tipperary saying to Tim, "Please don't cut her hair." Before going to university, she went to Goodmayes driving the Granada and went to the hairdresser. "Do your mum and dad know that you are having your hair cut?", said the hairdresser. "Yes" she said, "I'm going to university on Monday". The hairdresser put the cut hair in a bag for safekeeping, but I think, according to Katharine it has been destroyed now. Katharine read at Mass at Saint Bedes Church and the priest came looking for her the next Sunday- he didn't recognise her after having her haircut. Going back to the big car, Katharine was driving a group of friends going to a party, all wearing hats, and they were stopped by the police in Ilford, who wondered what they were up to. They soon let them go! While at the Ursuline she made many friends; one of them also had a parent who came from Tipperary. She is still in contact with them and 'zooms' due to the virus, being unable to meet up.

Music in the Family

When Katharine was around ten, we took her down to Essex to Mr Milne who played in the Frank Sweeney band. He played the piano accordion and taught Katharine. He informed us of where we could buy a second-hand accordion. I think it was in Ilford. Katharine did play it for a while, but it was far too big for her. It went up in the attic, where it stayed for 30 years. On a visit to Gresham Drive, Joel said, "Grandad, have you still got mum's accordion?" Tim said "Yes" and Joel asked if he could have it down from the attic. Down it came, and straightaway Joel played a Tipperary song: *Templederry My Home*. We were amazed, as he played by ear, with no music. Joel and Peter both learnt the piano. I'm not sure what grade they got up to. To hear them playing was wonderful. I think Joel still plays the accordion in his band and teaches some music at work now. All seven of us were taught music. I can play a little.

Pets

When Katharine was growing up, she was always fond of dogs. We did have two: Princess and Brandy. Princess was lovely. Danny's brother brought us to Romford market where we bought her for £1 (32). I said she was a small breed, but Danny said the stall holder "is telling you lies", thinking she would grow huge, but she stayed small. The only thing was that she moulted a lot and one time Father John, Tim's brother, was over on holiday wearing black trousers, and he was very annoyed at getting covered in white hairs. We always brought Brandy to Sheffield and he had the run of the garden. Dad and Brandy probably walked all of Sheffield. Whilst in Ireland we had to keep him tied due to traffic. He got cancer and we brought him to the vet. There was nothing that could be done. Dad and I buried Brandy under an old apple tree in Aughavoghill.

12 HOLIDAY MEMORIES

Ireland

Once in Ireland when Katharine was young, we went to Spiddal in Galway- all Irish was spoken there. Katharine loved the sound of the people speaking, and didn't want to come away. At the Blarney Castle in Cork, you were held over the edge of the tower by your legs to kiss the Blarney Stone, and I did that. It brings you good luck and the 'gift of the Blarney'. You were given a certificate- I will have mine here somewhere.

Tipperary

Just remembered- as you know the clocks go forwards and back in spring and autumn, and they always changed in Leitrim. But Tipperary did not change the time, and I often remember saying to dad (Tim Ryan), "Is this Tipperary time or Leitrim time?" Now they do change the clocks, but did not do so for many years.

We did go on a visit to Ireland every year, and Katharine had her case packed weeks before we went. Wellies were number one for her. One year, during the time of the hay saving in Tipperary, she was up on a haystack on the cart and slipped down behind the horses' hooves. Mick was in a dreadful state, as she could have been killed, but Katharine only laughed.

In Tipperary Katharine spent a lot of time with the children at 'The Cross' (33), who were second cousins of her own age. The festival in Kilcommon was a great function and was always full of people. In a big field there was a stage put up and all famous bands played there. It raised a lot of money for local businesses and for the church too.

The Missing Hat -another story, again in Tipperary: Peg Harrington, a cousin of Tim's, was going to her son's wedding and refused to buy a hat. I said I had a nice one belonging to Mam and posted it to her. However, I'd put the wrong name on- I put 'Peg Kennedy', her maiden name instead of 'Harrington'. Apparently, it was in the Post Office in Templederry for ages. One day Marion, her daughter was in the Post Office and the postmistress asked her if she knew anybody of this name, so the hat was claimed and Peg went to the wedding wearing the hat.

Leitrim

In the year of the big storm in 1987 we were over on holiday. We went out to Stracomer to visit Hugh, Rita and family. The lane down to the house was closed, as many trees had to come down and blocked it. Hugh and Tim set to clear it by cutting the trees with saws. When we went back to England, Goodmayes Hospital grounds were virtually closed: I think sixty-seven trees were down.

In Leitrim we did a lot of visiting and went to Garrison every week to a pub, 'The Lakeside'. They had a dance there and a raffle. I often won, but only small prizes. I remember going to an auction in Bundoran with Mam and Tim, and Tim saying "be careful". I put up my hand and got a nice piece of material: it may be still here in Sheffield.

Gorey Memories

We went on holiday with our friends, Danny and Eileen to Gorey, County Wexford, and had a wonderful time. Danny showed us all over Gorey and especially the graveyard. It was a great sight. He pointed out the graves of Travellers, which were wonderful. A lot of money was spent on them. Danny told us that when a Traveller's funeral was on, all the shops and pubs were closed. Danny's parents owned a bicycle repair shop. Danny had great memories of that and his growing up in Gorey. He took us to a special pub, Browne's (34).

Whilst we were in Gorey, Danny was up on the roof doing some repairs. He slipped off the ladder and down he went. Tim Ryan got some chalk and went out and drew a picture of a person on the ground (like a crime scene). Nobody knew what he had done. The following day Tim said to Danny, "Where did you fall from Danny?" Of course, we all went out to see what was going on! Danny never forgot that episode.

Some years after, we were in Gorey again; John and Alice were there too. We had been out celebrating and all the ladies wanted to go to the toilet on the way back. Danny stopped the car on a roundabout. "Get out" he said. We did and did what we wanted under the bushes on the roundabout! A lot of cars were going round…Danny told us that he had taken our photos….

The Boat Strike

Many years ago, when we were on our way to Ireland, as we approached Holyhead there was a big notice saying "Boat Strike in Holyhead". Eventually the road was closed as Holyhead was full, and so it was. We got Bed and Breakfast out on the London Road. There were a lot of us together, including Eileen and Pat O'C. We had a great time there. Eventually we got word that we had to drive to Liverpool, where the cars were all lifted by crane into the boat. The B&B lady only took half the money for our stay. Years after, dad and I were going to Ireland via Holyhead so we went to the place we stayed during the strike, but the lady there had died. We were given directions to another B&B, a Mrs Riston. Eventually we left a car in Ireland and we were collected from Knock Airport. At that stage we were spending a lot of time in Ireland.

Sheffield

When we visited and the boys were at school, we often collected them (a letter was sent by Katharine and Tim that we could do this. This was very advisable for safety).

We always came to Sheffield to be with Katharine and Tim for Christmas. Tim's parents also came sometimes. I remember Christmases when Joel and Peter were small. Katharine and Tim both do the cooking; it is always wonderful. Their friend from university, Father Chris visits also. As I'm now in Sheffield, it is a great party still. We exchange presents, have a lovely meal and drinks. Now Joel and Peter visit with their girlfriends too.

St Patrick's Day Joy

Tim and Katharine always cooked bacon and cabbage

whenever we visited Sheffield, especially for Saint Patrick's Day. It was a great meal, that we always enjoyed in Tipperary also. It was dad's favourite. More memories- I keep remembering all these things: over the years of St Patrick's Day celebrations with Katharine, Tim, and the boys, Jim and Shelagh (Tim Murray's parents) were also there sometimes. One year Katharine had done everything in green, white and gold. Joel was quite young with his lovely white curly hair. I can now visualise all the food arrangements in the Irish colours. We all wore St Patrick's day badges. Katharine announced that she was expecting a baby: that was Peter. We always had a great sing song. Jim was great to do all that.

Thank you, Katharine, Tim, and your two wonderful boys Joel and Peter.

Sunshine Holidays and Friends

Sunshine holidays from 1979 were all arranged by our great friend Danny, RIP. Four couples all went to Spain and other such places. It was great fun. Danny collected all the money; he would arrange transport to the airport; he collected all our passports and cases at the airport and we all went off and had tea or something stronger. We all had great holidays playing jokes on each other. Once Tim changed Alice's sun cream for yoghurt! Alice got burnt and was puzzled how this happened. She did find out eventually.

One holiday in Spain, Tim and I got to know this couple and the woman asked our names. When we went to the beach, she shouted, "here are the Reillys". We then introduced John and Alice and Danny and Eileen to them. I think her husband was a vicar. One day she was eating sandwiches and her mouth was full and she kept talking and it was not a nice sight. Tim said to John, "Joycie, give her a kiss". We did have a photo of her somewhere; her name was June (35). When we got home, Tim wrote a letter to Danny and signed it "June" and Danny and Eileen received the letter. As far as I remember there was somebody we knew going to Spain and Tim asked them to post it. Eileen hid the letter and can't know where she put it to this day!

One day on that holiday Tim went off walking on his own as he often did, and went to someplace up the mountain and hid a bottle somewhere. Then he went off to a big B&B and he told them what he was up to. He had all the information about this couple - their names and the name of the place. The following morning at breakfast he said, "I had a funny dream last night" and told them all about this place, the people, the bottle. He then insisted that they should go for a walk, so off they went and John found the bottle, as Tim had described! Then Tim brought them to this B&B and John asked them a lot of questions. Tim had the owners well set up. "That is like my dream" he said. Sometime after, our friends found out what he had done.

The last such holiday for Tim and I was to Playa del Inglés on the south coast of Gran Canaria. I wanted to go there again and told Katharine, who booked it all- I was delighted. This was all cancelled because of the virus. Someday we may still get there.

13 AUGHAVOGHILL: OLD AND NEW

Whilst we were still working at Goodmayes Hospital (Tim had returned there as a charge nurse when Fords in Dagenham was reducing in size), Hugh, my brother phoned us to see if we would be interested in a house and land for sale near my original home in Leitrim. We talked it over and bought Aughavoghill. Hugh did all the transactions. We then went over to Ireland and met the Rynn brothers, the builders in the Melvin Hotel, Kinlough and gave them the contract. As work was done, they informed Hugh and he paid them (we had written a letter for him to do this). As you see now, it turned out to be a great adventure. When we both retired, we spent six months of the year there, as well as time in Sheffield.

The River
Tim did a lot to the river running next to the house to make it nice: clearing it out, creating an island and making the bank grassy. Joel and Peter did swim there. Aiden, my brother painted and signed two nice paintings of the river in full swell. The river has fish in it -maybe salmon! Tim was always

chasing the heron as they were very quick to catch a fish. A neighbour, Brian did bring fish once in a barrel to the river, to increase the numbers.

I remember seeing tadpoles in a river in Tipperary. I had never seen these before; coming from the country and living near rivers and lakes you would think there were plenty there. I asked Tim before we came back to Leitrim to put some in a plastic jar and I brought them back to Leitrim and put them in the river. I thought these little things would grow to be fish- how foolish!

One time we were in County Meath with our friends, Myra and Austin, who kept ducks. They had a duck that was causing a great deal of problems, so dad put the duck in a paper bag and we drove it all the way to Leitrim. What a racket all the way. The following day dad put it in the river on a lead; the next day he went out walking on the road with the duck on the lead. A friend of Breda, my niece commented, "I've seen everything now- a duck on a lead". We have a photo of it on the river! Eventually the duck was cooked.

Farming Ways: Old and New

The way of farming has changed a lot. All work on the farms is done now by powerful machinery. Some years back when we got the house at Aughavoghill sorted, there was a large space vacant next to it. Tim commenced collecting all old machinery. Hugh knew where there was some old machinery abandoned as well. In those days Cathal bought up some farms and any old machinery found was given to dad. The two big wheels that made our wheel gate I think were given by some of the Foley family. We brought some pieces from Tipperary- pots etc., some of which are now in Sheffield. All the old machinery is painted in black; when repainting is needed, a neighbour, Jerry, does that. Aughavoghill was once his home: we purchased the house and land from his parents. Before they owned it, Hugh Charlie owned it. He had a nice orchard, the one we as children used to rob!

In previous years in Chadwell Heath Tim had got an allotment and grew lots of vegetables. There is a photo somewhere of them- potatoes, cabbage, turnips, carrots etc. Eventually he had to give it up, not having the time to look after it, and houses are there now. As I told you, when Tim and I retired, we spent maybe six months in Aughavoghill. Dad was very happy there and set potatoes. They were great and we cooked a lot of them. Tim gave some to Hugh to use as seed potatoes. He never used them, and they were at the stage of rot when we returned. Dad had to throw them away- that was the end of vegetables. He did sew lettuce once and was so proud of his venture, only one morning he went out and they were gone- slugs of some sort. Martina (Hugh Og's wife) told me of some methods to deal with slugs, and I've told Katharine.

The Rhubarb Garden

We brought a lot of rhubarb up from Tipperary out of Father John's garden. When Hugh heard of this he said "I have some down in a field and I'm not interested in them". Hugh brought them up to Tim and hence a wonderful crop grew across the road, opposite the hay shed. Dad cut a lot every year and put it in the freezer. I do remember one time Tim was not very well and I went over and weeded the patch. Now Martina wants to take it over. She is getting a man, Cormac, to clear the place out, which I'm delighted with. Tim did plant some rhubarb in Gresham Drive, which grew well. The new people there will wonder what it is.

Tim Ryan the Farmer

14 THE LOCALITY

Lough Melvin Again

Lough Melvin stretches from Northern Ireland to Kinlough, which in Irish is 'Cionn Locha', meaning 'head of the lake'. There are six islands on the lake; two of these are in Northern Ireland, including Bilberry Island. The Lough covers around 5000 acres, including the islands. The lake is seven miles long and three miles wide. Lough Melvin is renowned for fishing, with international fishing competitions held there. The last one is at the end of September. The boats go out from Breffni Pier at 9am and return there at 5pm. The fish are weighed and very large prizes are given. I've seen a boat being one prize, which was made in Tipperary – in fact Tim and I did go to see the man who built it. A large barbecue is put on for a small charge. A dinner dance held in a big hotel in Bundoran is also an important local event.

There are various types of fish to be caught there: brown trout, Atlantic salmon, Melvin charr (deep water fish, seldom seen), perch, rudd, as well as gillaroo ("red fellow"), ferox (up to 15lbs, eating brown trout and other fish) and sonaghan (black spots) strains of trout.

There are also eels in Lough Melvin. I remember dad (Tim Ryan) got to know two men who could catch these; they caught them near the old reeds in the lake near Stracomer. The first time I saw these the men brought them in a bucket full of water. They cut them up and cooked them. They gave some to Tim, and he said it was a lovely dish. I refused to eat them as I thought it was cruel. Some weeks after, Tim was not there and these men came back with more eels. They put them in a plastic bag- what a racket they made-I asked them to put them in the garage. The following day, Tim cooked them again. I think that this is not allowed now, as they are protected.

The magazine, *Trout and Salmon* often mentions Lough Melvin. Some years ago, I got to know a German man and his wife attending the fishing competition and asked if he could paint a picture of the lake. He did one for Dad and I, and one for Katharine and Tim. He did a lovely job of both of them. When I go to see Katharine and Tim, I always look at the picture, which gives me great memories of home. I have now received a great photograph of Lough Melvin, sent by my brother Cathal, taken years ago by a friend of his at 'The Resting Point', a place on the way up to the bog.

Legends of the Gillaroo
There are several stories about why the Gillaroo is in Lough Melvin, the only lake that this fish is caught in, in Ireland. In one version, St. Brigid was offered chicken to eat on a Friday as she walked through Garrison, County Fermanagh. She was so angry at this, as meat is forbidden on Fridays for Catholics, that she threw the chicken into the river, where it changed into a fish (36). It was found when the fish was

cleaned out, that it had a gizzard, which is only found in fowl. In another account, a monk on the lake shore who had been fasting, put an eel and a duck egg on a cross he drew in the sand, prayed and they turned into two beautiful golden bellied trout, which he then returned to the lake.

Rossinver, Our Saint, and a Noble History

I have an unpublished document about St Mogue (Maedoc/Aiden), *Where a Saint Lies Buried in North Leitrim* by Mr G.J. Fergus and Mrs M.B. Fergus Feely, written out for me in italics by a man called Eamonn from Barnsley, who worked at Goodmayes Hospital. The document draws from Plummer's *Lives of Irish Saints Volume 2* (37). Saint Mogue was told by an angel to go to Rossinver and build a church which he did, in preparation for his death and burial. In *The Annals of the Kingdom of Ireland, by the Four Masters* (38), Fergus is referred to as a 'coarb' to St Mogue: an 'heir' or 'successor', and in *Lives of Irish Saints* as "his own dear faithful foster child and equal -aged companion". Fergus accompanied St Mogue to Rossinver, where the Saint

"Placed the erenaghship [role of administrator] and high headship of the place under his judgement and warranty, and under the authority of his tribe and true descendants till the day of doom. He left grace of riches of entertainment, grace of liberality and large hospitality, grace of learning and intellect to his successors after him, and to the place permanently, if only they are submissive and respectful to Maedoc..."

In the death notice for Patrick Fergus it is noted that one of his last acts was to help the priest clean up and repair the old Rossinver Graveyard where he was "laid in the tomb where all his great ancestors lie buried, including his great kinsman,

St Mogue".

The church ruins are visible from the road, and St Mogue is believed to be buried inside the gate to the ancient graveyard. A new graveyard is now there too, with the land given by a local farmer. There is also Saint Mogue's well near a house at Gubalaun, on the lake shore.

Queen Maeve's Grave

Queen Maeve, queen of Connacht in Irish mythology, has her cairn on the summit of Knocknarea, Co Sligo. You will remember this day- Katharine, Tim Murray, Tim Ryan, Joel and Peter went up to the summit and had a picnic. Tim Murray wondered out loud what could make the glorious day and view even better, then Tim Ryan produced a hip flask, two glasses and a small drink of whiskey. It is a national monument and people should not climb it or take stones away.

Faith of Our Fathers

In the year 2000 we celebrated Mass on Church Island owned by Cathal, my brother, on Lough Melvin. There was a great turn out in spite of the weather, as it was a very stormy day. Before the day of the mass, Cathal had men to go out and tidy it up. We went out with my brother Hugh. It was a dreadful crossing: I said to him, "I won't come back with you- I may stay there all night". We returned with Joe, a neighbour, in his boat. There are the ruins of a church there. I suppose mass was celebrated there in penal days. I will try and get some history about it -from where or how? (39). MacClancy, who gave shelter to Francisco de Cuéllar from the Spanish Armada after ships were lost off the coast of Sligo, is reputed to be buried there.

While we were over in Aughavoghill dad always lit a small bonfire on the 23rd of June that he said was the feast of Saint John. It apparently was the custom all over Ireland years ago, though I don't remember it happening in Stracomer. I found out recently on the Internet via Facebook about the 23rd of June, Saint John's Eve, known as Bonfire Night, and about its ancient roots (40).

15 TIPPERARY TIM ACROSS THE DECADES

As you all know, Tim Ryan was from Knockfune, Tipperary and very proud of his birthplace. He was one of twelve children, so it would have been a lively household. When Tim came to England first, he stayed with relatives, Bab and Christie Riordan in Finsbury Park (Christie later was Katharine's Godfather and my Mam was her Godmother). Tim's first job was in a pub in Southend on Sea, The Master Johnston. That was long before I knew him. He later worked in The Three Rabbits Pub in Manor Park, in East London.

Some of Tim's family came over to our wedding. His elder brother Mick was living in the home place with his Mam and Dad. Mick later got married to Nancy. Tim went over and looked after the farm while they were away. They had two children Peter and Josie, and now Peter has two lovely children.

On my first trip to Tipperary with Tim, I was a bit apprehensive, but I was accepted by all the family. Tim's Mam and Dad were so nice and his Mam baked lovely bread in the oven, or maybe on the open fire- I can't remember. While Katharine was very young and still in a carrycot my Dad decided to drive my Mam, Katharine and I to Tipperary on a visit (I think Tim was in England). Even in a carrycot she was a bad traveller and was very sick. We got as far as Carrick on Shannon, South Leitrim, and my Dad was going to take us back to Stracomer, as she was so sick. We carried on to Tipperary and all were delighted to see her. My Mam and Dad always talked about how the Rosary was said every night in Knockfune.

On one of my early visits to Tipperary, we came across a large crowd on the journey south, somewhere in County Limerick. A band was playing and the people were dancing. It was called 'Crossroads Dancing' and the dance area was a wooden platform (41). We did not have this in Leitrim, but it was all over Tipperary, Clare and Limerick.

We would travel every year to see family in Clare: The Quinns in Ennis (Nora and Paddy who went on to have eight children) who owned a pub, on to Limerick to see the Hurleys (Biddy and Brian) who owned a tobacco factory making 'Sweet Afton' cigarettes, and then Peggy and Bernard in Power's Pub, Clarecastle, who went on to have eleven children. All the family were very welcoming and I was well accepted. Peter, Tim's younger brother was still at home on our first visit. He later married Freda. Her family owned the pub in Silvermines, Tipperary, so Peter became a publican. On Easter Sunday, before daylight Peter, Freda and their children would go up to a high hill nearby to see the sun dancing. I doubt if they do that now, as like me age is catching up with them.

Dad, Tim Ryan, told a great story. He was travelling back to

England once, and Customs were always on the lookout for illegal alcohol: poteen (poitín). The poteen was often coloured with a few drops of tea to make it look like whiskey. At the Customs you had to open your case to have it ready for inspection. Dad opened his case to find two dead pigeons, which he managed to throw on the floor before Customs arrived. This was done by his brothers Peter and Mick!

Another brother, Father John is a priest who spent time in Australia and Texas, before returning to Ireland. Winnie married in England and had three children (42). Josie, another sister married in Canada and had one son, Christopher. She visited Ireland regularly and went to Medugorje in later years with Peter and Freda. Annie married Andy, a neighbour from nearby Kilcommon, who owned a pub in Dublin, and went on to have five children.

Like his projects in Ireland, such as renovating the old farm machinery, Tim Ryan had projects in England too: you may all remember people used to have wooden bead car seat covers. Well, Tim made sets of rosary beads out of them for all the Fergus and Ryan families. He spent hours making these out in the garage in Gresham Drive. He got all the extra holy pieces, such as crosses, in a religious shop in Ilford. Katharine and Tim: you were given some.

He loved making links with his young life in Ireland, such as at Easter, dad always ate a goose egg from a special egg cup, which I've kept. He would not buy the egg from Romford market: we went out in the country and found a farmer that kept geese.

Tim was a wonderful husband and father and he was over

the moon when the grandchildren arrived. We were all in Ireland for some birthdays of dad. Joel and Peter wrote out a menu for his 70th birthday and got his breakfast ready (I still have the menu). They sang 'Happy Birthday' to him as they presented it. A great surprise for all!

When Mick died, dad and I went to Tipperary with Annie and stayed in their house in Silvermines. Katharine came over to the funeral- we didn't know she was coming. She didn't know where we were staying and so slept in her hire car at the end of the boreen at Knockfune, after arriving about 2am. She then went up to the house in the morning and Nancy told her where we were staying. We were shocked when she came to the door in the Silvermines.

Tim Ryan was very well-known and liked, and that showed at his funeral, which had a huge turnout. He had said to Katharine, "if I die before mam, I want to be buried in Kinlough". That was his wish. A coach arrived to his funeral in Leitrim from Tipperary. Three priests, including Father John were on the altar. The reception was in the Allingham Hotel, Bundoran arranged by Hugh, my brother. It was closed at the time, but they opened the hotel for Tim. Tim's 'Month's Mind' mass (43) was arranged by the family in Curreeny church. Myself and Katharine flew to Dublin and went down to Tipperary with Annie for it.

16 TIME TO MOVE

Tim Ryan died during heart surgery in October 2006. I lived in Gresham Drive for approximately ten more years. This was my choice, and what I wanted to do at the time. I carried on with voluntary work in the local MS unit and SENSE shop, and kept up with great friends and neighbours. When Tim died, I called John and Alice my 'English Mam and Dad'. They visited me often; each Sunday, they collected me for dinner, and I often stayed over with them. I had my accident on Grove Road, falling on wet leaves in 2014, sustaining fractures to my leg, shoulder, arm and wrist. I was admitted to Queens Hospital, Romford (which replaced Oldchurch Hospital where I trained), but don't have much recollection of it. I was then transferred to King Georges Hospital, Chadwell Heath (on part of the site of the old Goodmayes Hospital). I was very well treated and spent nine weeks there. A patient now, instead of a nurse. Katharine stayed for a while then travelled up and down twice a week to see me, whilst working full time; Tim and boys were up and down to visit me- it was time to move. It was time for a change.

Katharine and Tim did all the buying and selling, as I was not able. They sold the house in Gresham Drive, where I had lived for sixty-five years, and bought me a wonderful flat, with the lounge looking out onto the Peak District. It was the best move I ever did, arriving here 2nd of November 2017. When I arrived with Katharine and Tim, I first met the Development Manager, and she took all my details. I think Tim was here to meet the removal men and Katharine and I followed by car. I spent a few nights at Katharine and Tim's home whilst they sorted out my flat. I have a lovely home, with bedroom, bathroom, lounge and kitchen. They had done all before I came: the bath taken out and replaced with a walk-in shower, my furniture arranged, and the two large cabinets. When I walked in here, it was like the lounge in Gresham- the china, glassware all in place. I asked Katharine, "how did you know where to put the things?" She had taken photos before the removal men came and set out my flat accordingly. All my clothes were hanging up in the wardrobe; the carpets and curtains were cleaned. I am very well cared for by Katharine, Tim and boys, including all the visits to restaurants. Katharine wrote out a list, and I've been to forty cafes and restaurants so far! I'm very happy here: so near Katharine, Tim, Joel and Peter. I should have done it years ago, but I wasn't ready then.

I think I have covered all my bits and pieces. It is a big mixed up. I'm giving it to Katharine to sort it out. Thank you, Katharine. I hope Joel and Peter will get a chance to read it and make note of what Granny did in her lifetime. Thank you, Tim and Katharine, for all you did for me.

17 SHEFFIELD

New Friends in and out

When I first moved into the Development, I was invited to go for tea and biscuits in the lounge at 3pm: it was a great way to get to know all the residents. In the beginning I was very apprehensive being outside in a strange place, then Katharine got me a 3-wheeled trolley -well it was great: on the bus (five minutes' walk) to town; go to daily mass in the cathedral; then to Marks & Spencer, or Lynne's Pantry (introduced to me by Peter) or John Lewis, or go to Greggs for take home lunch. On a few occasions I got lunch free from Greggs, as they said I was a good customer! I used to do shopping in Marks and Spencer or Tesco: very handy for the microwave or oven. I got to know a lot of people at Mass and on the bus.

When I came to Sheffield, as I said, I went on the 51 bus each day to 'town'. That's what they call going into Sheffield, rather than saying 'the city'. People would speak to me, and as soon as I spoke, they would say, "you are Irish", then tell me that their great grandfather was Irish, for example. It was only then I realised I still had my Irish accent! I met a lot of people, now friends, going to the bus. There is a lady near the bus stop- she phoned me and today brought me a lovely bunch of flowers. There is this girl- I only know her as Rachael (44) and she knows me as 'Maureen'. She is about thirty years old and uses a wonderful wheelchair. One day last week I got a lovely card from her and she had signed it "Rachael, the girl in the wheelchair at the bus stop". She had the wrong flat number, but the lady who got it delivered to her flat passed it on to me. I was indeed very touched by this card: It brought tears to my eyes. Today I looked out my window by chance, and there she was going past on her way to the shops. We had a chat -how wonderful!

Medical Care and Services

Medical care is first class, and I'm delighted with the GP Surgery that I was registered at. Before my arrival at the Development, Katharine put my name down with Manchester Road Surgery: excellent. On my first visit I was seen for a consultation with a GP who sorted out the medication I was already on from Chadwell Heath. Now I ring for repeat prescriptions, and they are delivered from a local pharmacy. There I go by the name Mary Bernadette, but the receptionists know my name is Maureen. If you need to see your GP, appointments are given on the day you phone. Walking there causes me to be breathless, so now I go by taxi (45). Of course, that was before the "virus". Now if you need a GP, they may speak to you by phone, if a face-to-face appointment is not required.

Katharine put my name down for the "School Road" dentist, as all the family are with them. There again: very good. On my first visit to the dentist in Ballyshannon as a child, presumably with bad toothache (no such thing as check-ups then), I got as far as the dentist's chair. As soon as he approached, I was off and out the door, pursued by my parents! Tim Ryan talked of pliers as the remedy in Tipperary …

Spectacles: Katharine asked me to get an eye test. I was checked at Boots in Sheffield and needed two pairs- reading and distance. Hearing aid: I was tested by Judith in my flat and got my hearing aid very quick.

Hairdresser: Dawn comes to a lot of people in the Development. I see her every six weeks. Due to the virus, she couldn't attend, so I gave my hair a good chop. So, you see by all this that I have all under control.

Weather Memories

Last night 16th of June 2020, we had an absolute thunderstorm, with rain, thunder and lightning. Some boys were playing football on the flooded field across the road. As children, when we had lightening, we would go under a table to hide, which could have been dangerous. These boys kept playing their game.

18 MY EYEPAD [*SIC*]

My EyePad, given to me as a birthday present by Katharine and Tim when I was 83 in 2017, turned out to be my lifeline (46). At first, I could only use it to look at photos that Katharine put on, and I now have all sorts of wonderful ones: lots of photos of family members, friends, outings, holidays. Katharine has taken up growing vegetables "like her dad", and I have great pictures of her displays of produce. For birthdays it is lovely to meet up with the family for a party- Katharine, Tim, Joel and Peter. Shelagh, Tim's mum, is there sometimes- she lives in Cumbria. I have all the birthday photos on my Eye Pad.

Click on, Keep Touch and Join in

I now keep in touch with all the Irish news, listening to Ocean FM, the local radio station for the North West, back home in Ireland, every day; and the news on RTE, the Irish television channel. My Irish relatives reckon I know more about Ireland than they do! I also use FaceTime, Facebook, Facebook Messenger, BBC iPlayer, ITV hub for catch-up on Coronation Street, and do Zoom chats with John, Alice and Eileen. I 'zoomed' into the Joyce family quiz every week for a while, with all twenty-four of them; it was lovely as during this virus we are not able to visit. John and Alice's children had called us 'Uncle Tim' and 'Auntie Maureen' and now the grandchildren called me 'Auntie Maureen', which is very touching. One night, one of the grandsons who is only eight, said "Auntie Maureen I would like to play you a tune on my violin". He played on the screen, was very good we all clapped for him. Eileen was zooming too and said she would like to give away a keyboard belonging to Danny, as none of her grandchildren were interested. When his twin heard that he said to his mother "I would like to learn to play keyboard" so that was going to be passed on. Tim was his mother's Godfather, and I am Godmother to his aunt.

I use Facebook on my EyePad to talk to friends in Ireland and Australia. My friend Ann Fergus, mentioned above, married Nick Rogers and emigrated to Australia. I just get her name- click it and there they are! Technology is wonderful, and I'm only a learner. The young people of today are geniuses. A member of staff, Val, retired from Goodmayes Hospital and set up a Facebook Group, "Pensioners from Goodmayes". I'm now a member and can log into about twenty retired staff. All of them thought I had retired to Ireland.

Of course, it is still great to write and receive letters. I correspond with someone who came to Goodmayes Hospital as a junior doctor, and now sits in the House of Lords as a Baroness, helping to formulate new Health and Social Care legislation.

Mass

I had been going to daily mass at the Cathedral in Sheffield. On Sundays I was collected by Katharine and Tim to go to

Saint Vincent's Church in Crookes. The priest, Father Paddy is from Kilkenny. All churches of all religions are now closed. Most churches have put mass on the Internet. I watched daily mass at 11am in Kilcommon, Co Tipperary, with Fr Woods. He went there as a young priest, and he is now 78. I spoke to him on the phone and he told me after he was ordained, his first parish was in Yorkshire. He had great praise for the bus drivers as they never took money from the priests. That is now changed, I suppose.

On Sundays I have a big choice: Saturday evening mass 8pm Kilcommon, Sunday 9.30am St Edward's Church in Romford, then Sligo Cathedral on Ocean FM, or Saint Bede's Chadwell Heath 11 am, so you will gather I don't have time to go for my walk on a Sunday, but still do my exercises from the physiotherapist.

Radio Fame
One day I heard on Ocean FM that Leitrim were playing a football match in Croke Park, Dublin. I rang in to the radio station and got to speak to Francie Boyle, the presenter. He asked me a lot of questions; I didn't know that it was all played live on air as an interview until Breda, my niece, rang and told me. I have heard the recording on my EyePad, and can listen again. I only rang to wish Leitrim all the best!

19 LOCKDOWN AND A NEW HOBBY

The Virus

When all this is over and a lot of us are not here anymore: Joel and Peter -your families will ask a lot of questions. This virus has changed all our ways. Joel and Peter, I'm sure you will keep all this in your heads and remember all about the effects of the virus, and the impact on everybody. For a time, Katharine could only visit on a Monday, doing all my shopping and cleaning, full of energy. I continued contact with nice friends in the Development via phone, as we could not meet.

Reading and Other Irish Lives

I've just read a book, *an unconsidered people the irish in London* (47). I really had a good life compared to some people coming from Ireland to London. Joel, my grandson, wants to read the book next. I'm now at the ripe old age of 86. During the last ten weeks we are on semi -lockdown because of the virus. We can go out for short walks, but I decided to stay put and with time on my hands I would start Reading. I have not read since during my years of study, when reading was very important. I've now read seven books and tomorrow start number eight. I like short stories or books with chapters; when I see a book with a large number of pages and no breaks, I think, "that's not for me".

I've been reading a book by Bill Cullen, *It's a Long Way from Penny Apples*, given to me by Tim Murray, covering his journey from an early life of poverty in Dublin in the 1940s, the fifth of 14 children, selling things on the streets from the age of 6 (48). Bill Cullen recalls his grandmother, Molly Darcy talking about the potato blight, a fungus-like disease that from 1845-1852 ruined the potato crops. The grandmother had worked with a man who lived through those times and she told her grandchildren how only potatoes were affected: wheat and barley were fine, which meant their prices doubled. The fish in the lakes were owned by the English, and if an Irishman was caught fishing for them, he would be flogged for poaching. Molly named Sir Charles Trevelyan ['Lord'], who allowed the export of the grain abroad, telling the grandchildren that today it would be called genocide. I did tell Katharine how I well remember my Dad with a special can on his back, spraying the crops against blight, up and down the potato ridges. This mixture contained water and bluestone (49). It may not be done in these days.

Molly told them "That dark desperate chapter in our history left a million Irish people dead on the land, and another two million who left for foreign shores" (50). She told how many people died on the voyage on 'coffin ships' and were thrown into the sea for the sharks; of mass evictions, with whole families destitute. The poor land in the west had already been branded in Cromwell's time when Irish landowners were dispossessed and told to go "to Hell or Connaught" (51).

Thousands had to emigrate, and for Molly, the song *Danny Boy*, though written by an Englishman, captures the sorrow of the mother waiting for her son (52). Molly wonders how Ireland, known as 'The Land of Saints and Scholars' (53), with druids and holy men living all over Ireland, could have been brought to such a state.

I have also been reading on the Internet about the Famine in Ireland (54). I did go to the Ulster American Folk Park in Omagh with Marlene and my sister Pat many years ago. It tells the story of the millions of people who left Ireland on a dangerous voyage to a new life in the 18th and 19th centuries. The Folk Park was a very interesting place but sad.

20 LONDON REVISITED

In 2019, on Bank Holiday Monday in May we went to Essex -all booked by Katharine. On our way we visited Betty, who had moved to be near her family. Then off to Romford. The hotel was great and was near the Market. I had lived in Romford sixty-five years and never knew there was a hotel there. I suppose I never needed one. We attended Mass in Saint Bede's Church. Father Martin was away in Rome. I met a lot of people I knew, then we were off to the Eva Hart Restaurant and had a great meal. Katharine had arranged to meet friends in Collier Row Club: John and Alice, Eileen and Eileen, Jim and Nora, Maria, Wally. It was a great reunion to see them all. After a late night and back to the hotel, we were taken out the next day by John to a Chinese restaurant out in the country. We went on to Gresham Drive to Khalilah, and family. She had baked a special cake. Then we saw Satnam. She and her family are Sikh. When we went to visit, Satnam started crying. I asked why she was crying and I was amazed at what she said: "Since you have gone, we don't see anybody. You kept us together". We visited George and Sylvia who were nice to us when we were looking at

Gresham Drive, showing us around their house when we asked them. We saw Mary, and Adrienne who was then in the process of moving. There was no answer from our old house, and I thought the place looked neglected. Katharine said, "Mum are you sad leaving Gresham?" I said "No, and I'm glad to be going back to Sheffield".

21 THE IRISH ROAD TRIP AND A SMALL WORLD

In September 2019 Katharine booked a trip to Ireland. It was great; all the hotels were wonderful. First stop was Dublin and we saw Annie, Tim's sister. Milo, husband of dad's sister Mary RIP, had just died, so we met his family. We were treated to tea and cakes by Josie, daughter of Mick RIP, Tim's brother, at The Red Cow Hotel on the outskirts of Dublin, then on to Tipperary to see all nieces and nephews.

We visited Curreeny Church, where the family would have gone to mass all through the years, and where the family graves are. A car stopped outside, and it was a cousin of Tim's who had been at his funeral. We went to the Prayer Garden Kilcommon Church, a wonderful place. Father John had put an inscription on the old family grave. It reads "Maureen Fergus married to Tim Ryan 31st of March 1959". We went on to County Clare where we met Ada Power, daughter of Peggy RIP, Tim's eldest sister, and other members of the Power family in their pub in Clarecastle. We met up with Quinn cousins, children of Nora RIP, Tim's sister, in Ennis and Lahinch. The only family we didn't manage to meet were any Hurleys, children of Biddy, another of Tim's sisters. Leaving Clare, we went to mass in Knock, where I had the Blessing of the Sick.

It was then off to 'lovely Leitrim' where we had one week. Katharine and I visited the Great Northern Hotel in Bundoran, Co Donegal for a cuppa. We were told that Marion Fitzgerald, from Ocean FM was next door, entertaining a group on holiday from Tipperary. The cousin we had met by chance the week before at the graveyard at Curreeny Church was there in the group with his wife: again, it's a small world. Marion came out and we had a chat with her. She asked where I was living and when I said "Sheffield", she said "I will put you on my list on Ocean FM". Now every Sunday I get my name mentioned during her programme! On our return journey to Dublin, we called at Castle Blaney, County Monaghan, the home of 'Big Tom', from the country and Irish showband, 'Big Tom and the Mainliners', my idol over the years. I had photos taken with his statue and sat in the chair sculpture there. A great trip throughout.

22 THINGS HANDED ON

The christening robe worn by my Dad was handmade by an aunt, Sister Mary Aloysius, of the Sisters of St Louis, Bundoran. Dad was the first of the family to be baptised in it. His date of birth was registered in Ballyshannon as 28th February 1906, though was recorded as 27th February on his Belleek China Christening mug, now in the care of my brother Cathal. Katharine also has a Christening mug given to her by my Mam and Dad, as their first grandchild. I was baptised in the robe, as were Katharine, Joel, Peter, and many cousins, as well as other babies of friends. One of Veronica's twins wore it. When I gave the robe to Veronica it needed some mending. She did a great job and the robe looked amazing when she finished it. She then got a special box and gave it to Bernie Regan, her sister, RIP. The latest to wear it was Bernie's grandson Zack, on 6th November 2016. It is a shame we did not keep a record of all the lovely babies who were baptised in it. One of the family may be able to do this, which would be wonderful. The robe, as you will gather, is over 110 years old and is as white as the day it was made.

So, there you have it: begun during the first Lockdown in 2020, here is my life story and journey from home in lovely Leitrim to here in lovely Sheffield, that I learnt about in school so many years ago. Joel and Peter, you will know that my growing up was very different to yours. Now, you have both chosen professions that help others, like this Irish Nurse did: I am so proud of you both, as your grandad was too. You both have a love of Ireland, and that, as your granny, is wonderful, for wherever I am, 'home' will always mean Leitrim. A Miss McGowan of Kinlough (55) wrote a poem of emigration and farewell around 1856, recalling all the beauty around the lake, still unchanged now:

**And when I do return again those scenes I will review
We'll dance and sing the life long day round Melvin's
Water's Blue.**

23 BIBLIOGRAPHY AND NOTES

(1) Dad: in the original writings, 'Dad/ dad' is used to refer to Charles Fergus, father, and also to Tim Ryan, husband. For clarity throughout, 'Dad' will be used for Charles Fergus and 'dad' for Tim Ryan.

(2) Vincent Gormley, *The Gormleys of Ture, A Short Family Tree*, 2016.

(3) Benedict Kiely, *Drink to the Bird*, 1991. P.101.

(4) An Altar Stone, Bog-fhód (Buckode) | The Schools' Collection | dúchas.ie (duchas.ie)

(5) The Dobhar-chú or King Otter is a creature of Irish folklore. It resembles both a dog and an otter, though it sometimes is described as half dog, half fish. It lives in water and has fur with protective properties. A headstone, found in Conwall cemetery in Glenade, County Leitrim, depicts the Dobhar-chú. The stone is claimed to be the headstone of a grave of a local woman killed by the Dobhar-chú in the 17th century. https://en.wikipedia.org/wiki/Dobhar-ch%C3%BA

(6) "Grief-stricken by the sight of Jesus on the cross, the donkey turned away but couldn't leave. It was then that the shadow of the cross fell upon the shoulders and back of the donkey, and there it stayed. All donkeys have borne the sign of the cross on their backs since that very day." Sue Weaver, *The Donkey Companion* (Storey Publishing, 2008).

(7) "**Fairy forts** (also known as *lios* or *raths* from the Irish, referring to an earthen mound) are the remains of stone circles, ringforts, hillforts, or other circular prehistoric dwellings in Ireland." Fairy fort - Wikipedia See photo of Denny Sheerhan with Gerard Haran, who as a child at Buckode School collected 13 of the records in the Schools Collection at *dúchas.ie,* including *An Altar Stone* above, and another on Fairy Forts. His brother John, also in photo, collected a record on *Buying and Selling*.

(8) From Old Irish cúairt ("tour, circuit, circle").

(9) "Poitin dates back to at least the 6th century, an ancient farm-based spirit that's made in a single pot still, and takes its name for the Irish word for 'little pot', *pota*." Everything You Need to Know About Poitin, Irish Moonshine (theculturetrip.com)

(10) John Gilroy: A Giant | dúchas.ie (duchas.ie)

(11) As a child, I remember being introduced to various people around the area and local village. Granny would say "This is .... I brought him/ her into the world."

(12) The Stations: "This tradition dates back to the Penal Laws, when it was forbidden for Catholic priests to say Mass in public. To get around the problem, the Mass was often celebrated secretly in people's homes, and afterwards, those in attendance stayed on for breakfast. This was often followed by a full day of merriment - but only after the priest had finished his breakfast and taken his leave!" An old custom that still exists...The Stations - World Cultures European (irishcultureandcustoms.com)

(13) Wren Boys: History, Heritage, Folklore, and News from County Sligo, Ireland (sligoheritage.com)

(14) Mummers: The local dances at Christmas tide were called 'Mummers Dances', but they did not seem to involve the tradition of visiting actors and performances elsewhere in Leitrim where mummers dressed themselves in straw. These masked singers continue an Irish Christmas tradition | National Geographic

(15) "Children had their very own Irish Easter traditions known as the clúdóg. This involved calling on neighbours and family to collect gifts of eggs, potatoes, cakes, bread and butter, and milk or flavoured water. The children would then gather in a field, a makeshift 'den' beneath a tree, or a fireside (if the weather was poor) to cook their eggs and enjoy their feast." Irish Easter traditions - how our ancestors would have spent the holiday (irish-genealogy-toolkit.com)

(16) The Cure: What's it like to have the gift of 'the cure'? - BBC News
The original draft stated, 'The Cure was', and was then changed to 'The Cure is'.

(17) Colman Rushe, *The Things We've Handed Down,* 2019.

(18) "...nobody told us": they could have been going to/ from Derry, further down the coast.

(19) Carrigans was the centre of a major flax and linen producing area, possessing one of the largest flax mills in County Donegal.

(20) The surrender of German U-Boats and Operation Deadlight at Lisahally, Co. Londonderry - WartimeNI

(21) The Missionaries of Africa (also known as "The White Fathers"), are an international Missionary Society of priests and brothers, founded in 1868, by Cardinal Charles Lavigerie, Archbishop of Algiers and Carthage in North Africa. The name "White Fathers" comes from their white habit. This was based on the traditional North African dress of a white gown (gandoura) and a white hooded cloak (burnous). https://www.missionariesofafrica.org.uk/our-story

(22) Castlepollard: Castlepollard mother and baby home was opened in 1935 and closed in 1971. During that time, 4,972 women were admitted; 4,559 children were born there or admitted there. It was

owned and run by the Congregation of the Sacred Hearts of Jesus and Mary https://assets.gov.ie/118624/03b4e442-a027-4e1e-a9ef-27d17850ebf6.pdf

(23) 'Thunder': more likely the Irish pronunciation as ''tunder' amused him.

(24) "There was a great Irish club in Romford, the *Shandon*. It's long closed down, now. A great Irish dancehall. You had two hospitals there, you had Oldchurch, and then you had a TB hospital called Rush Green, and so you had all the nurses there. I used to go with a nurse from Cork, there. Aw, Jasus, a great dancehall it was. Gone now. All the bands of the time used to come — *Big Tom and the Mainliners" Showbands and Dancehalls. Interviewed in his room in Arlington… | by jim mccool | Bhoys of the Big House | Medium*

(25) Irish dancehall called the "Blarney Club" in the basement of 31 Tottenham Court Road, under the *Gala Berkeley Cinema*.

(26) Cauliflower, 553 High Road, Ilford IG1 1TZ. Grade II listed building, built on an old market.

(27) BCG vaccination: vaccination protecting against tuberculosis.

(28) Lyn Wilson, *The History of Goodmayes Hospital 1886-1989,* P. 17, 1989

(29) Child of Prague: "When it was vital to have good weather, like on the day of a wedding* or a rick, the little statue of the Child of Prague, normally kept in the house, was moved outdoors and placed under the hedge." The Infant of Prague Irish customs - World Cultures European (irishcultureandcustoms.com)

(30) Kalilah: family names changed for confidentiality.

(31) Kishorn: When 3,000 men were drawn to the Highlands to work for up to £2,000 a week | The Scotsman

(32) Our friend Danny Grannell, from Wexford.

(33) 'The Cross' was a shop, pub, undertakers and farm combined.

(34) Browne's,Gorey:https://www.irishtimes.com/business/commercial-property/baritone-publican-with-deep-roots-in-the-trade-1.977776

(35) 'June': name changed for confidentiality.

(36) Gillaroo legends: Gillaroo - Wikipedia   Lough Melvin (en-academic.com)

(37) C Plummer, *Lives of Irish Saints* Vol 2, 1922, P 256. Fergus' genealogy is given as "son of Oilill, son of Eiten".

(38) *Annals of the Kingdom of Ireland, by the Four Masters, from the earliest period to the year 1616. Edited from MSS. in the Library of the Royal Irish Academy and of Trinity College, Dublin, with a translation, and copious notes, by John O'Donovan. Dublin, Hodges, Smith, 1854.* Volume 3, P2.

(39) Church Island (Inis Teampuill**):** The History & Heritage of Rossinver – Rossinver Youth and Community Project

(rossinveryouthcommunity.com)

(40) June 23rd: is St. John's Eve or as it is known in many parts of Ireland, Bonfire Night. It was traditionally marked by the construction of large fires throughout the countryside. These were lit at sundown and were the focal point of communal festivities. St. John's Eve or Bonfire Night; Irish Folklore | Irish Archaeology

(41) Dancing at the Crossroads: Balinvreena C - Visit Ballyhoura

(42) Father John died December 2020, aged 92. Winnie died November 2021, aged 91.

(43) Mass is traditionally celebrated one month after the death of a person.

(44) Rachael: name changed for confidentiality.

(45) By taxi: walking more regularly has built up stamina, so taxis are no longer needed.

(46) My EyePad: spelling of iPad has been preserved from the original, as it reflects its role as a new way to look at the world and out in to the world from the flat.

(47) Catherine Dunne, *an unconsidered people the irish in London*, 2003.

(48) Bill Cullen, *It's a Long Way from Penny Apples*, 2001.

(49) Bluestone: bluestone (sulphate of copper), washing soda and water.

(50) Bill Cullen, *It's a Long Way from Penny Apples*, 2001, P106.

(51) To Hell or Connaught: Act for the Settlement of Ireland 1652 Act for the Settlement of Ireland 1652 - Wikipedia 04.03.2022

(52) Danny Boy: Danny Boy: what are the lyrics and history behind the traditional Irish song? - Classic FM

(53) Land of Saints and Scholars: Aoibhinn Ní Shúilleabháin: The scientific origins for 'saints and scholars' (irishtimes.com)

(54) The Great Hunger: Great Famine | Definition, Causes, Significance, & Deaths | Britannica

(55) Old Songs Never Published | dúchas.ie (duchas.ie)

ABOUT THE AUTHOR

Maureen Ryan, nee Fergus was born in the rural north west of Ireland in County Leitrim. With a tradition of being able to trace ancestors back to the time of St Mogue (Aiden), the family was and is rooted in the locality of Lough Melvin. As a child she was sent to live with her grandmother to keep her company for six years, just visiting home for holidays. On one such occasion a younger sibling asked her mother who this girl was who kept coming to stay, only to be told, "That's your sister!" Maureen returned to the shores of the lake to attend secondary school and then, like many others, left to train as a nurse in England. As well as a great sense of vocation, working with patients in a large psychiatric hospital, after general nurse training, Maureen found love there and forged many deep friendships. This book, though often addressed directly to family members, is ultimately a love letter to life and to Ireland.

Printed in Great Britain
by Amazon